THE **DI** **BARBARIAN** OK
TO **ROMAN BRITAIN**

𝔓eople to meet and places to plunder

"𝔗he essential handbook for tourists and pillagers"
Julius Caesar

"𝔄 modern 𝔑omℭom"
Constantine the Great

"𝔍 never go raiding without it"
Childeric the Sluggish

Lee Rotherham

www.BretwaldaBooks.com
@Bretwaldabooks
bretwaldabooks.blogspot.co.uk/
Bretwalda Books on Facebook

First Published 2013

Bretwalda Books
Unit 8, Fir Tree Close, Epsom,
Surrey KT17 3LD

info@BretwaldaBooks.com
www.BretwaldaBooks.com

ISBN 978-1-909698-07-9

Bretwalda Books Ltd

Foreword

by Hrothgar the Despicable

Pillaging is a tough line of work. You spend half your time rowing to somewhere swampy, hide your boat somewhere where it takes hours to find it again afterwards, and then have to run round the countryside like a mad thing to grab your trinkets and livestock before the nearest guard force comes haring down the road after you.

This book is a real help. Nowadays, I while away my hours crossing the northern sea picking my spots with care, safe in the knowledge that I can park in a nice sandy beach only a quick hour's jog from some unsuspecting person's villa.

And if you can't read it, it has pictures in.

But life isn't just about leaving the family behind and going and knocking down someone's town. Some of these places are really quite attractive, full of the high points of the leading civilisation of our time.

So whether you are a trader looking at exploring new opportunities for enterprise; or a wise man tracking down some of the leading people of the world in order to converse with them as they visit these shores; or even a pupil being taught the ways of the earth, this is the book for you.

Britannia. A land of marvels. A country of opportunity. Provinces of the greatest empire the world has ever seen.

And all marvellously flammable.

Whether you come to Roman Britain looking for plunder and fighting or for trade, this is the book for you.

CONTENTS PAGE

An Introduction for Barbarian Tourists

Travellers in our times are not easily drawn to Britannia, or Britain. Why should they be? Civilisation (in the physical form of the Romans) has arrived relatively late here. Neither Hercules nor Dionysius wandered these parts in their mighty travels. Unlike with most of Gaul, the country refuses to fully assimilate into the Roman way. The land is isolated, being rather distantly connected with the great shipping routes of the Mediterranean. Its rumoured riches that drew the attention of the first Caesars have failed to materialise, leaving it a constant drain on the resources of the state, which has to pay to maintain a sizeable, underemployed and therefore dangerous standing army.

Plus it rains a lot.

Further south, on the other hand, and all is culture. Ancient Greek colonies can be found as near as southern Gaul and Eastern Spain. Beyond there of course you have the real treasures. Of the Seven Wonders of the World, most are still in existence. In Egypt, the Great Pyramid still stands sentinel. The Statue of Zeus at Olympia remains a site of marvel. The Mausoleum of Halicarnassus reminds us of a past great king, and the Lighthouse shines on over Alexandria. Not all is well. The shell of the Temple of Artemis wrecked by fire still looms over Ephesus. Of the distant Hanging Gardens, reports suggest ruin, and the Colossus of Rhodes has long now been laid low by earthquake. But even with this partial list comes a massive number of beautiful and ancient cities spread out across these shores, bedecked with sculptures by the greatest artists of all time, and rich in the accumulated wealth of centuries of royal power and imperial might.

At the heart of this empire of course lies Rome. While over time the true seat of power may vary, as rulers settle in Milan

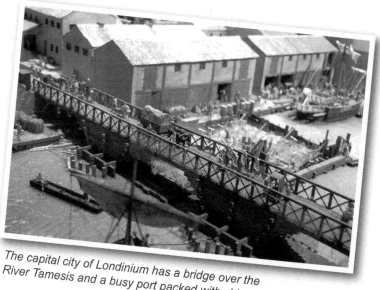

The capital city of Londinium has a bridge over the River Tamesis and a busy port packed with shipping.

to be nearer the empire's borders, or Ravenna or even in Sicily, to be more secure when they are breached, Italy remains the great jewel. It long remained the source of its manpower and the enduring reserve of its legions. Even as its political and military importance shrank over the years, it remains the heart of what it means to be Roman. Rome became Italy, and Italy was Rome. With a population perhaps of ten million at the time of the invasion of Britain, it was perhaps six times Britain's at the time, and three times even at its height. Sitting at the heart of the Empire's trading routes, if you have money it is truly the place to be. It is where the finest glassware meets the best jewellery, and where olives meet myrrh. It's warm. It's well-ordered, with a strong legal tradition. It was for much of its time peaceful (barring the occasional civil war). It is at the heart of political power, where careers as well as fortunes are made. The best architects, poets and artists of the era are drawn there. A number of places come a fairly close second, but Italy is the place to be.

Yet despite these obvious attractions, Britain does have a lot to offer.

Your average barbarian visitor has a number of preoccupations and interests that make the island particularly endearing, even if it remains under-explored. For starters, as a barbarian your motivation in pursuing a career in the Roman civil service is likely to be nil, as are your chances. Both will pick up over time as Roman civilisation and security teeter, and men of quality are sought to defend the Roman way of life even if they aren't Roman themselves. Some will even come to Britain and feature in the island's history, though sadly often as little more than footnotes. We'll introduce a few you might bump into during your travels in the course of the book.

Rain is a constant threat in Britain. Try to find a modern Roman-style building with a tiled roof if you can.
Photo: Edal Anton Lefterov.

Since you are probably not looking for a lifestyle change or career move, there is also the possibility of a little illicit jobbing on the side. As the Empire grows weak, there will be plenty of opportunity for plunder. With a wide coastline, the local army can't cover everywhere at once. With a few boats and a small band of hairy savages, particularly angry hairy savages, it is relatively easy to put the wind of their new-found god up the locals. Note that they have a tendency to run off into the middle of a field and bury their extensive silverware in a pot, so speed is of the essence in your raiding.

For more peaceful types, later times allow for settlement. Having all these lunatic hell-raisers coursing around the place may actually encourage the local magistrates to let comparatively friendly old you and your family settle locally, in return for helping out with defence and the local economy. So if you are a farmer with problems at home, perhaps later on you might start to consider getting on board a boat and starting a new life in the distant colonies.

For traders too, Britain offers prospects of wealth. You might find things cheaper going direct to North Gaul, since imports from the south have shorter distances to travel. But there are a number of products that Britain does have to offer that are of reasonable quality and where it may be easier for you to ship them home.

Finally, of course, there is what the land can offer the student. Roman Britain is not like back home amongst our fellow barbarians, where the high point of existence is a bit of beery arm-wrestling, a midnight prance about some old stones and hoping you don't end up sacrificed in a bog. It may not be the highest of the high culture; Tacitus and Seneca aren't present in person having a chat about aspects of "Socratic dialogue" in the original Greek. But if you go up as far as the very border posts on Hadrian's Wall, you'll meet Roman guards who know their Virgil, and quote it. Rome is here.

Whichever barbaric tribe you come from, from the frozen north, ostentatious east, or extremely lost west, you'll find something in these islands for you. Whatever your interest in Roman Britain, whether as a trader, a student or a professional or amateur pillager, this book will help steer you round a very alien society. It'll take you to some wonderful, imposing and beautiful places, which you can gaze on admiringly before you burn them down.

Life in Britain provides us with a remarkable insight. It's truly a unique culture, half-Roman, half-Celtic, and half-barbarian. Yes, it gets complicated later on.

Planning Your Visit

Tourist Seasons

Arranging your visit to Roman Britain is a tricky choice. Every season has something special to offer.

In the high season (from around AD 43 to AD 180) you can witness the height of the Roman experience. Set in densely populated countryside from even before the Conquest, Roman towns are growing and then flourishing. Trade expands. Theatres and amphitheatres spread across the land, allowing visitors access to the highlights of the not-so-ancient world. Despite some periods of civil war, these mostly take place far away and lead to minimal destruction and third party burning to interfere with your holiday arrangements. This is a silver age holiday ideal for silver age holidaymakers.

Mid-season (say AD180 to AD 370) and there are rocky periods. Occasionally, accommodation is patchy as civil war kicks off, sometimes with Britain as the starting point for a little provincial insurrection. The importance of the island waxes and wanes. Sometimes it is at the very heart of all that is Rome, as Emperors come to wage war in the north of the island. Two great emperors are even proclaimed here in these very shores during this period. But this is also the period of slipping decline. The territory is divided into smaller provinces in their own right; and the island forms part of smaller imperial patches as the great empire is occasionally broken up into two or four to make it more manageable. Travelling during this period can be more exciting and there are fantastic people to meet, but it can also be less comfortable for more exacting travellers. The great villas for example no longer provide the same sort of accommodation opportunities as of old, and are often replaced with more basic amenities.

The low season by contrast (perhaps AD 370 to AD 478) is ideal for backpackers, particularly those that bring their own transport, such as a raiding ship. The last great flourish of

Roman culture does not end with complete and sudden extinction, however. Roman forces are mostly withdrawn first as part of the ongoing civil wars of the period, and then to fight off persistent barbarian threats on the continent. Roman reinforcements do briefly cross the channel to support what remains of local government, but the country splits and power is fragmented. The great towns decline. Trade becomes more difficult, and merchants reading this book may be more inclined to barter with contacts amongst the new barbarian settlers in the east than take their chances with the sub-roman world in which old rules and laws are often arbitrarily upheld by petty tyrants. Coins become rarer, and even if the move outside of direct rule from Rome around AD 410 still leaves a lot of quite wealthy people around, what's happening over in Gaul and beyond makes everyone nervous that the whole system is going down the drains. But it is an exciting time all the same, and provides opportunities for settlers seeking new lands, plus plenty of hiring opportunities for professional soldiers who want to keep well away from the highly dangerous fighting that involves Attila the Hun over in northern Gaul. Even after direct rule from Rome ends, some embers of Roman existence continue to glimmer in the West of Britain, and reward the patient traveller with a hint as to what has been lost in this new pan-Barbarian age. Note, however, that currency becomes rare: yours will be valued, but be prepared to barter.

As we go through some of our profiled spots, you'll also find a box with information in italics. This is for the benefit of those poor people who can't visit Roman Britain at all, because they have to come out of season, in the twenty first century. Things aren't so wonderful by then. You'll have to dig for your Roman memories. But there are still traces of the old magic, and students who are gifted with a hint of imagination and understanding will be lucky enough to gaze on some ancient treasures.

Highlights

1. Temple of the Divine Claudius at Camulodunum
You'll only be able to see it for a few years, because it will be burned down before you can barely utter the words 'pillaging mayhem'. But the temple of the deified Claudius in Colchester shows what a classic temple from the height of the greatest empire the world has ever seen looks like when it's erected to impress the natives in the new capital of the land. Time your visit carefully, otherwise you'll be caught by the revolt and trapped inside waiting to be butchered by Boudicea's ravaging mob.

2. Visit to a bath house
Romans take their cleanliness seriously. But it's not all madness with a loofah. Explore your sensitive side, as well as your sensitive parts, and take a couple of hours out, exercising and relaxing with a large number of completely naked strangers. It's an experience you'll never forget.

3. Celtic Britain
Across most of the continent the Celts are a lost people, but traces of their culture still survive and even thrive across the British isles. Fancy trying on a mad helmet with huge horns on? Want to chat with a druid about the magical properties of mistletoe? Like to try your hand in a chariot? Askdirixions not to some remote village in Northern Gaul, but to the remoter spots off Britannia, where fascinating alternative cultures exist beyond the Roman Pale.

4. Big huge stones
No one knows who built them. Possibly they are the work of the giants, trolls or titans, but these huge monolithic structures dominate the landscape. Many sites are scattered across the land and can be seen as you pass along the western route,

including a massive henge and a mound of earth the size of a small pyramid. Marvel at these huge ancient things that some locals claim their ancestors built ... as if!

5. Triumphal arch of Ritupiae

Ritupiae is the gateway port into Britain, and chances are you'll enter the province passing right through a massive triumphal arch that matches anything the imperial heartland has to offer. It's huge, it's in your face, you are meant to be seriously impressed ... and you will be.

6. Northern frontier

I sing of arms and the man ... so began Virgils's epic poem, the Aeneid. You'll find plenty to sing about when you visit the edge of the Roman state: a mighty military complex guarding one of the construction wonders of the age, a wall built on the command of a Roman Emperor. Some say as man-made objects go, it's so huge it can even be seen from a very long way up by seagulls. But only make the trip in peace time. Come war, and the last place you'll want to be is anywhere near one of the legionary camps, talking foreign.

7. Shopping in Londinium

Whenever you time your visit, Londinium is a must-see location. It's one of the earliest Roman conurbations, and while you'll have to time your visit to avoid Boudicca's, at least you'll have some advanced warning to head out of town if you time it badly (there's a ship leaving with the governor for Gaul in twenty minutes). On the other hand, for most of the rest of the time you'll find an important city that is a major political power centre, on the trade routes across the Channel. Want the latest in continental fashions? Come to the market stalls of Londinium: you certainly won't find them on the frontier!

8. The Eboracum of the Emperors

The city some might call York is the backbone of the northern defensive hinterland. As such, it's the base for many an expedition into free barbarian lands, and headquarters of a mighty army that at its height includes three standing legions straddling the north. Given the need for occasional offensive action, it's not surprising that Emperors and other VIPs (victorious imperial purplewearers) have trod these very streets. Time your visit well and you can meet some of the most important people in world history, and share an oyster with the movers and shakers of most of the entire known world, ruling the destinies of millions.

9. Julius Caesar on manoeuvres

Before Britannia was a province on the map, before Rome even was an empire with an emperor, there was Caesar! Meet him during one of his excursions into southern Britain. Watch the unstoppable force of nature as he meets baffled failure and is defeated by nature, discovers seas with tides, a serious lack of plunder, and lunatics on wheels. It's a rare setback for Rome's number one trouble maker and future god.

10. Remembering Rome

Fancy a discount break in the Low Season? Bring your friends out plundering as the Roman Empire collapses around your ears. Travel west where the Celtic experience survives and outlives all-conquering Rome. Or come and visit the east coast with your family: you'll like it so much you'll want to stay. The magic of antiquity lingers on, even when the Empire has formally shut shop and has been overrun from Spain to Sicily by lunatics with spears. Britain offers a slightly quieter corner for plunder, free from marauding Huns, Vandals, Suevi, Visigoths, Ostrogoths, Burgundians, Franks, Alans and a host more of hosts. Or you can bask in the reflected glow of a sunset culture and chill out with the sub-Romans as they cling on to their ancient way of life and memories of glory days, offering up your services as a mercenary. Avoid women with swords in ponds. Terms and conditions apply.

Britons can be a snobby lot and refuse to invite a barbarian like you to a feast. You will find a large axe works wonders for gatecrashing.

Getting there

Britain is an island, part of a group of islands that sit to the west of the continent of Europe. These are the Orcades, Acmodae (Shetlands), Hebudes, Mona, and Monapia (Man), plus the tin island of Mictis. You will need a boat. It is highly recommended that you use a vessel with sails rather than a coracle, as unless you are crossing from the side nearest to the island, you will probably drown.

Travel is safer in the summer season, owing to kinder seas and there being less chance of fog to hide the stars, which you will need to navigate by.

Crossing from within the Roman Empire, you can seek passage on one of a number of merchant vessels

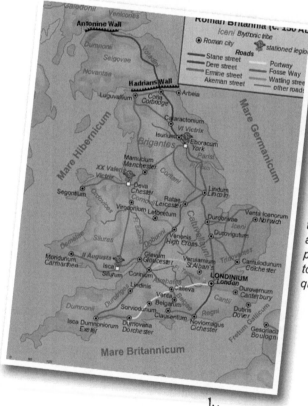

The network of roads makes getting about Roman Britain a doddle. Unfortunately it also allows the army to respond quickly to any trouble, so if you are here for plunder stay close to your ship for a quick getaway,

that ply the trade routes between the major ports. As with all sea travel, the safest passage is typically the shortest. Those with connections may be able to pull strings and obtain space on a ship doing an official run with imperial messengers, although there are repeated moves to stamp down on abuse of the imperial postal service. Shipping involved in counter-piracy patrols might also provide a route across, though there is no guarantee of the harbour you will end up at, and in periods of heightened tension your motives might be questioned. Coming from the continent, we recommend heading straight by land for Bononia (Boulogne), and trying your chances with one of the captains who may have space.

Of course, if your intention is raiding then you will already have your own vessel, and the entire coastline is there for you to pick your spot. Note, however, that as raiding increases you will find a series of 'Saxon Shore forts' being erected in the south east of the country to keep an eye open for ships such as yours, and to summon troops if you land. Getting some local insight on beaches is therefore very handy if you decide to make a night time landing to dodge the first patrols. There are plenty of wide, open shingly landing spots across the south, and sandy bays in the east. Avoid the area around Dubris (you may know it as Dover) as this is both perched on the edge of massive white cliffs, and the home of a significant naval presence. Several other forts are also dotted up the coast in the third century, including Regulbrium (Reculver) in the bottom of the bay of the river Tamesis and Branodunum (Brancaster) monitoring the entrance to the Wash. Opening times vary from season to season, with several closed by the end of the fourth century, so check local timetables to avoid disappointment.

Bononia as we have indicated is a major port, and is the headquarters of the Roman North Sea fleet. This is a sizeable threat and you will be chancing things to head far into the British Channel with the war drums beating. Even small patrols can be a major challenge, especially since the prospect of loot is not so great. From a distance, with the men well hidden, you might with a cheery wave pass for a trader when travelling alone, but expect to be closed upon for checking, and be treated as hostile if travelling in company: particularly if there are a lot of you. Keep the noise down, the maniacs out of sight, and the sails fully hoisted, and you might be in luck and pass a vessel already on task. If not, your best chance if you can't outrun her is to board as quickly as you can rather than face missile fire and, in a really bad case situation, having some burning bitumen in a pot dumped on you by a small catapult.

Travel to smaller islands off Britain that fall within the Roman orbit can typically be arranged through local fishermen. More difficult is getting to Hibernia, the second main island in the group that lies to the west of Britannia. Chances are that you will not be interested in going there, as it is a bad-tempered island of constant fighting and less profit. Some trading expeditions do go there and your best bet again will be to seek advice in Bononia before departing for Britain proper. Alternatively, in the low season you can wander the shoreline in the west of the country completely unarmed, and wait to be picked up and sold into slavery in Hibernia by their marauding pirates.

People have been coming to these shores since they were known as the Cassiterides, or islands of tin. Early descriptions see Britannia as a three-pointed isle. Of the triangle, the promontory running towards Gaul and the Hercynian Forest is called Cantium. The part running at the second tip of the triangle along the Roman shore is called Belerium. The tip that lies running towards the frozen seas is called Orca. Pytheas of Massilia sailed these parts at the same time that Alexander the Great was doing his thing in the East; his reports provided the basis for reports on the geography for the better part of the next four centuries.

Happily as we were planning this book, we bumped into a well-travelled captain of a merchant ship in a bar. He drew us this map on the back of an old sheepskin. He was drunk while he did it, very drunk, but even if you treat it as very approximate it's a huge improvement on a map we saw by Julius Caesar that makes Britain look like a wedge of cheese, and another recent one where the island appears bent over with stomach ache.

Weather

Compared with other lands this far from the midday sun, the island is relatively warm. The reasons for this are not known, but suggest Britannia faces more out westerly into the ocean than some maps indicate, tucking in beside Hispania (Spain). Though visitors from sunnier places find it very cold under the stars of the Great Bear.

There are four main seasons, during all of which rain is a persistent menace. The sky is permanently hidden by clouds.

Experts who have measured these things declare that in the far north in particular, days here are longer than in Rome. There is light in the night time, since there is nothing to obstruct light from still reaching the high sky in these flat and empty parts, and in the furthest north but a slight difference between night and dawn at all as you watch the sun neither rise nor set but merely travel across the sky.

Temperatures vary from hot to cold. In the summer months, ensure when travelling you have enough liquids, ie stop to replenish your water skins when passing streams. In winter, particularly the exposed terrain in the north, the winds can get very biting. Snow can fall in some quantity. Not for nothing do some call it the island "rigid with ice and cold, far removed from both lands and the visible sun." However, the land is spared the worst extremes of northern frosts.

Happily, the more established buildings have what is known as central heating. Gaps are left under the floors and in the walls for heated air to circulate, thus increasing room temperature. If you go and have a look how they do it, you might spot a local oddity. There is a type of marvellous black rock dug out of the ground locally that catches flame and burns with a ruddy glow giving off heat, and this is sometimes used.

Strong winds, storms, and lightning can be encountered. Fortunately, there are a large number of shrines and altars that can be used to keep the gods happy for when you are out and about.

Note that for repeat visitors, you may notice a change over time. In terms of temperature, you might spot a tiny increase around AD 300, then a gently sliding drop. You may find increased rainfall in the fifth century, leading to increased risks of flooding and difficulties travelling. You might also observe a drop in general temperature, and an increased level of public anger in general as they become seasonally depressed more easily, such as if crops fail. At the same time, you may over the long years also notice the sea level going up by several feet. Some talented sorcerers have calculated a rise of over two feet a century from the moment the Romans appear, perhaps thirteen feet over the whole period of empire, meaning extra earth and levels of props that keep needing to be added to water fronts and coastal roads.

Of course, such predictions may be alarmist. But they might explain why you need to take a bigger step off the boat next time you're in harbour. Just be aware of the possible dangers your pillaging can have on the environment. Think of all those flooded coastal communities back home you're forcing to up sticks and move into Roman lands. Have a social conscience. Try a smoke-free sacking. Take the 'burn' out of slash and burn.

Britain in Outline

Geography

Britain sits, depending on your source, either thirty or sixty miles off the mainland where the Belgae live, opposite the lands of the Murini. It stretches out from there along the rest of Gaul and down opposite to Spain. Before the Conquest, its existence had long been mere rumour to other lands, though sufficiently so to have attracted waves of settlers over time if forgotten legends are to be believed, and boats from the eastern Mediterranean seeking rare tin.

We now know that the place is an island, an observation reported by the ancient Greeks but never entirely believed, a detail suspected in Caesar's time (who thought it triangular), rediscovered in the time of general Agricola, and confirmed by the expeditions of Severus. How it happened was a fortunate or unfortunate discovery, depending on whether you were part of the explorers. A group of soldiers press ganged from Germany rebelled, murdered their officers, and attempted to escape by sea. The waters and then the wind pushed them round the coast and back to their home lands, though not before having sunk to the necessity by hunger of eating some of their own number. The uneaten escaped to their homes, from where some were later returned to Roman territory thanks to the slave trade.

The reports of their journey proved a sensation. Agricola repeated the experiment and his voyagers confirmed he was on an island. They also for the first time related sightings of the Orcades, and reported in the distance a sighting of far-off Thule, normally hidden by winter.

It is a large island. It has been compared in shape to an oblong shield or to a battle axe, though some say the comparison properly works only when looking at the Roman portion. Variously, its length is reckoned at 951 miles, and its maximum width is reckoned at 308 miles, though others suggest 800 and 200 is nearer the mark. Around half it is said is held in Rome's name.

It lies at the furthest extent of the world, and in old times was counted as half beyond it.

Beyond the Roman estates, a large block of land juts out in the shape of a wedge. The seas in these parts are said to be heavy and respond badly to the work of the oar or even to the work of the wind. It is supposed the reason for this is the absence of mountains and land so that tides are slower.

It is a land of forests and swamps, not just in the far free north, but even in the south. True, over time visitors will note man's hand marking the landscape, for instance in the east where the sea is beaten back by ditches and land reclaimed from the ocean – a wonder of technology, and worth seeing if Roman ditches are your thing. There are broad plains, fertile hills, mountains fit for pasture, all bedecked with flowers worthy of a picture such as writers say are like the jewels worn by a bride.

As you might expect, you won't find olives growing here, and both the food stuffs and the oil need importing. You might, depending on when you visit, find vineyards as far north as Eboracum. Commentators say of the land that it produces crops abundantly, ripening slowly but growing quickly thanks to the water in the ground and in the air. There is some gold and silver noted, though not in huge quantities. Thanks to the extensive shores, oysters are available, and these produce pearls albeit of an inferior dull blue colour. There is no pearl diving industry such as you can find in the orient; they are simply collected on the shore.

But overwhelmingly and despite the fields of corn, cattle and sheep, Britain is a place of woodland. Many small and gentle rivers cut across the landscape, now marked by small bridges where the island's Roman roads cross to connect the key towns. The landscape has many clear springs and cool, fresh lakes.

Two great rivers are also of significance. These are the Sabrina (Severn) and the Tamesis (Thames), and both provide routes by which foreign luxuries can be imported into the heart of the country.

Britain has, depending on who you speak to, between 20 and 28 cities, all of reputed handsomeness. Some, such as Eboracum, Deva, and Isca, are garrison towns. Four towns are colonies – Eboracum again, Camulodunum, Glevum and Lindum. Others are smaller market towns, and some fortified places with high walls, strong gates and imposing buildings.

The island is linked by a road network. These are primarily to allow soldiers to move more quickly, but are a substantial improvement on the old tracks which were far more limited in their spread and less useful in bad weather and in particular for anyone having to move something on wheels in winter. You'll find the east and the heart of the country criss-crossed like a web, with routes also running to the south west, and more running up along either side of the spine of northern hills approaching the frontier, reuniting to accompany the Wall. Some barbarian travellers have given them their own special names, to mimic the via appia or via domitiana over in Italy. You'll find Stane Street linking Londinium and Noviomagus in the south. Portway links Londinium with Durnovaria alongside it. Ermine Street runs from Londinium to Eboracum and the military north; Dere Street continues it from Eboracum to the northern frontier. The Fosse Way runs at an angle, from Lindum to Isca. Watling Street bisects this like the other part of an X, stretching from Dubris to Deva. Numerous other roads cut across and allow for connections. However, don't expect good connections or indeed much of a roadwork at all if you move far off the beaten trail, particularly in the west of the country and away from any significant population centre. Here you may need pack animals if moving goods, though note even using the roads in winter can be an issue for animals.

Less is known of Hibernia, the large island further west. It is smaller than Britain, but still bigger than Rome's other islands. It lies between Britain and Spain, and sits usefully for travel from Gallic ports. In soil, climate, and the habits and temper of its inhabitants, it is very similar to High Season Britannia, only with more cows and deeper bogs and no decent roads to steer you out of them. Some trade takes place with it, producing reports of an island of warriors and petty kings, all subordinate to a High King who must retire if he ceases to be physically perfect, such as if he loses an eye. Much more than that is guess work; if readers travel there, which will probably be with traders on its eastern coast, do get in touch and we'll include your discoveries in a future scroll.

Tribes and tribulations

If you come in the High Season, Roman Britain offers a rich diversity of peoples. The peoples have always been said to be simple and as such free of vice, rubbing along with one another quite well. True, it's essentially a bag of Celtic peoples, but the differences between the tribes point to different seasons of migrations from the continent. Put someone from the east in the same room as someone from the west, and you can tell them apart. This is all the more so with the differences between the 'free' Britons, keeping up with their ancient traditions, and those living in the Roman Empire.

The Caledonians of the far north, our Roman observers noted, have red hair and large limbs, suggesting to them they may be of German origin.

The Silures, who live in the west and mid west, have curly hair and are darker skinned. For this reason, and the reason that Spain is opposite, have suggested an Iberian origin.

Those that are opposite Gaul are taken to be of Gallic origin. Of the three, this at least seems likely. Though Romans also suggest that perhaps the climate has made people the same on both sides of the channel.

Taken as a whole, the Britons are said to be taller than their Gallic neighbours, with darker hair and looser build, a good half foot taller than your tallest Roman. They are, however, widely held to be bow legged and uglier.

In Caesar's time, it's said that the most civilized of all these nations are they who live in the south east, a heavily maritime district. Cingetorix, Carvilius, Taximagulus and Segonax are four of their leading rulers, with Cassivellaunus as a High King in the making.

They have most of the same customs as you can find in Gaul, though cheese making has had to be imported. Most of the inland inhabitants do not sow corn, nor do they for that matter have gardens, but live on milk (lots of it) and meat and wear skins. Dye is very popular, with a blue that comes from wood, making them look more frightening in battle. They wear their hair long, and shave their whole body apart from their hair and moustache. Up to a dozen men are said to share common wives, even between brothers.

What has certainly been noted since then is the effect of conquest on people in Gaul and Britain. These latter have kept their independence longer, and it shows. While the languages differ slightly, there is the same level of derring-do when danger approaches, and the same fear when faced with it. However, the Britons show more spirit, as they have only lately been living under a peaceful regime, and have not yet lost that warlike edge when they "lost their courage along with their freedom". Note, however, this level of aggression while it is increasingly sapped amongst the residents of Roman Britain, will very much remain beyond the frontiers for long years to come. So remember to show more respect when you travel outside of the provinces, as you may find fights break out much more easily, like home.

Britons you'll note endure cheerfully the conscription, taxes and the rest imposed on them, providing there is no oppression. It is said of them in the first century that "they are reduced to subjection, not as yet to slavery," and that they are impatient of such yolks. It's a trend you might see retained, contrary to expectations. By the low season, the Britons have forgotten their old tribal differences, and even when you see break downs in power, it's not to the old tribal structures locals will turn. But they will still keep something of their old independent spirit, plumping for leaders so they can do things their own way. It's not for nothing the third century sees Britain called "a province fertile in tyrants". They may be plumping for tough rulers, but they are their own rulers.

But these aren't the only Britons. Beyond the legions live the Caledonians and the Maeatae, and other tribes merged into these. The Maeatae live to the south nearest the Romans. Both tribes live in wild and waterless mountains, and bleak and marshy plains. They have neither walls nor great towns nor agriculture, but survive on livestock, game, and some fruits, avoiding the huge and endless supply of fish that abound. They live in tents without clothes or shoes, share their women, and bring up the children communally. They run their affairs mostly in a democratic manner, choosing the boldest to lead them into their favoured pastime of plundering.

Come later, and you'll see a bit more of a mingling, what

with people having come to live here from as far away as Syria. There'll still be girls wandering around Eboracum that you'll be able to spot by their auburn hair. Your blue eyes as a German interloper will continue to mark you out, though.

The tribes of the north are a funny lot. They make useful allies on a raid, but be careful to check they have not stolen your share of the loot afterwards.

26

Making Preparations

What to Bring

Britannia is a part of the Roman Empire and as such has a great selection of traders and stores able to sell you most of your comforts from home, and more importantly many of the comforts you have never even heard of before.

There are limits. During the early period of occupation, the Roman authorities took a harsh view of the druids, considering them (rightly) from their experiences in conquering Gaul as closely associated with the national identity of their new subject peoples. The extent to which the old-time druids practised human sacrifice remains contentious. There are suggestions that Roman historians such as Julius Caesar egged up reports to make their enemies look bad, just as their ancestors made great play of claims that the Carthaginians spent every other weekend immolating babies to their gods. So while reports have been made of giant wicker figures, packed to the brim with sundry sacrificial livestock and even humans, there is a flip side. Nothing has been reported to us of conversations Cicero and his friends also had with a rather civilised druid who popped up in the city of Rome by the name of Diviacus. The long and the short of it all is that the druids were quickly cooped up in an island called Mona, which after a vicious battle involving all manner of supernatural weirdness the legions then stormed.

In turn, this means the traditional apothecaries of society were hacked to bits. Even in Gaul, where their suppression has been less forceful, they are a thing of the past since Augustus banned Roman citizens from attending their ceremonies, and Claudius outlawed them completely.

So you might therefore want to consult your own priests before coming, and bring your own stock of traditional herbal remedies. Graeco-Roman medicine is very good, but its greatest physicians weren't looking for special roots amongst the weeds in these climes and would have no idea what mistletoe is for.

As for travelling comforts, thick furs will be unnecessary for most of the year. If you have a spare pack horse or slave with a wicker basket, pack a rug for extra bedding. You may be put up on an item of furniture known as a bed, and for those used to sleeping on the ground this can take some getting used to. A white pelt is a rarity in these isles and brought with you may also serve as reserve currency if you need some extra cash.

Weapons will be frowned on in civilised areas with a strong guard presence, particularly large weapons such as swords and spears, which suggest malign intent. Unless you are travelling through an area of notorious danger, all residents are supposed to seek official permission before being allowed to carry arms. If your intent is indeed, malign, then throwing axes make handy accessories for when people attempt to flee, and remember to bring along a few archer friends to keep heads down if you need to batter down any gates. On the other hand, if you are visiting peacefully, a concealed knife or

Most Britons in Roman Britain are civilians. Useful for trading with, and even better for plundering as they tend to run away from hairy barbarians like you.

packed weapon "for hunting purposes" will see you through nicely. Remember, once out of the city gate, the woods can be just as wild and dangerous as back home. Just make sure you are not caught armed without something in writing.

There's no need to pack your own food stuffs more than for when you expect to need for out camping. With the exception of tasty snow stock such as reindeer, which aren't native to Britain, you'll find plenty of fresher variety including most of the meats you'll be used to. Obviously you need to carry out the usual hygiene precautions before you eat, namely stabbing the dish to see if it moves.

Pack sensibly, unless you are planning on hiring animals or a cart. Porters may be available, though remember these may well be free men and therefore a station above dealing with slaves. Expect by Diocletian's day in the third century to budget for 20-25 denarii for an unskilled worker per day (meals excluded), to up to 60 if hiring somebody with practical skills, and 150 for a specialist. As a comparison, a pound of beef, a pound of cheap fish or a pint of standard wine would set you back 8 denarii.

Timeline

Timing your visit is everything. Who wants to arrive with a ship load of furs to find your usual customers are besieged by a cohort, and have more pressing things on their mind (like a catapult bolt)? Why come and visit at any old time, when you can meet and greet some of the greatest figures in all of history? Time your visit well and it won't be just any old vacation: with the eyes of the whole world on the neighbourhood, it will be the experience of a lifetime.

So whether you are planning just a quick boat trip to stock up on some duty free before the Romans quite get here (since they do like their taxes); or if you just want to get the autograph of an emperor, you'll find the following summary timeline of key dates in Roman Britain a must-have accessory.

In each case, the date of Britain's emperor is given, who may not be the same person that the Senate over in Rome would have you think was the legitimate ruler. As politics in places like Parthia is of no consequence for our visit, and involves just prissy people on horses riding around firing arrows at each other all day long, we leave out events in distant provinces where Britannia is not involved and we stick with the important local history.

It gives a very useful timeline of what happens, when. For now, the key thing to note is that you can time your visit to coincide with a number of very important events, to witness the key players first hand. Here's our top twenty to get you started.

Twenty Moments in Time

Julius Caesar briefly invades in 55BC and 54 BC, a display of the clash of civilisations.

The age of conquest: AD 43 onwards, Emperor Claudius comes in person, and along also come at least two other future emperors, Vespasian and Titus, with a pack of leading senators. 11 British kings are subdued.

Fightback: AD 60. This is the period of the catastrophic revolt of Boudicca, following in the path of the heroic and doomed resistance of Caractacus, where you can see the conflict through very different eyes.

AD 69-70, when British legionaries take part in the shocking fighting in north Italy that will settle who finally succeeds Nero. It's not their candidate, but the winner is Vespasian. The empire in Britain then expands as the troublesome Brigantes client kingdom is squashed.

AD 83, the battle of Mons Graupius and the high point of the Roman Conquest of Britain. But the far far north is allowed to slip from their grasp and the island remains forever after disunited.

AD 122 and a brief visit by another Emperor, the great Hadrian, who orders a huge wall to be built. Twenty years later, and an Antonine Wall is briefly occupied further north.

AD 193-197, and an Emperor made in Britain! Clodius Albinus the Governor is one of four claimants. He is nearly successful, but loses out to Septimius Severus.

AD 209-211 Four Emperors come to Britain. Severus brings his two sons, the future emperors Geta and Caracalla, with him to the island, and along with them comes another relative Elagabalus who in his turn will become emperor too. Severus dies before getting his fractious sons to learn to get on. With their father dead, the blood feud begins.

AD 261-274 Britain joins the north west of the empire in going its own way. Five local emperors rule Britain as part of the Gallic Empire, before the authority of the government in Rome is finally restored.

AD 276, Britain and the west supports one candidate for emperor, while the east supports another. British soldiers are amongst those that travel to the orient, then grow fed up and kill their man. Putting things in order again, Emperor Carinus then comes from Rome to campaign on the British frontier again, a full-blown ruler seen in person for the first time in generations. He secures the border, but won't last long.

AD 285, ruling becomes complicated. The empire is clearly too big and running it gets shared. Diocletian splits the empire. It was a neat idea that allows for an organised way to sort out who succeeded to the throne after an emperor died, but sadly doesn't quite end up that way in practice. For starters, Diocletian has competition...

Britain goes it's own way: AD 285-296. Carausius and Allectus rule in Britain as the 'British Emperors' before Constantius I comes over to settle accounts.

The pivot of history. Constantius is back, with his son Constantine, in AD 306. But he dies at Eboracum. Forget the rules about declaring a successor: the troops declare for Constantine: the path towards greatness is begun.

The purple returns. AD 343, and Emperor Constans arrives to quieten the border.

A British Emperor! Magnentius, whose father is local, runs the empire west of the Alps over AD 350-353. But support for him leads to horrible repercussions for many leading Britons when the hand of Rome returns.

AD 364-7: a barbarian conspiracy. Britain slips from the empire's hands, and great efforts are needed to restore control.

AD 383-388, Magnus Maxentius grabs Britain and the west. This is the last show of a strong empire, but already the signs of disaster are present, with barbarians at the heart of the army and entering the counsels of the throne room.

AD 394-5, the final encore. Under Theodosius the Great, the Empire east and west is briefly reunited for one last time. For a few last months, Britain once more belongs to the same entity as Carthage, Damascus and Constantinople.

AD 406-9 - Backing alternatives: the legions in Britain support (and then drop) three usurpers in a row. The last one, Constantine III, makes a go of it, with the support of his veteran and very capable lieutenants Edobinchus (a Frank but resident of Britain) and Gerontius, a Briton. But Gerontius becomes dissatisfied with his lot and grabs Spain, while the barbarians pile in too. Back home, the Britons locally sort out their own defences and 'undertake many dangerous enterprises' – having done so, they cast off their loyalty. Constantine's defeat removes hopes in Rome of finding someone capable of standing up to the Goths, rather than a leader who when he's told Rome has fallen thinks the messenger is talking about a pet chicken. The Emperor Honorius sends the leaders of the Britons a letter urging them to defend themselves as best they can since he has nothing to spare, a letter not unlike those that have gone to other cities across Italy even, but full of deeper meaning to an increasingly cut-off society. It's the symbol of the end.

Playing by different rules: With no official Roman military presence from around AD 410, Britain is 'in the Roman Empire, but not run by the Roman Empire'. Welcome to sub-Roman Britain; culturally affiliated, but run by local councils. It's a final game changer. Yet in a sense, when the rest of the Western Empire is gone, the spirit of the Empire lives on here in one distant corner.

Visas

Travel permits are not required, which is just as well given a lack of reading and writing in Germania. In the unlikely situation where you are travelling to Britain from a distant province, you may find some form of paperwork useful when crossing administrative boundaries between different emperors.

A note of introduction signed by an administrative official might also be useful for gaining a place on any official shipping. On the other hand, you might expect access to be very difficult in times of warfare or civil war, and particularly during periods of barbarian tension. In these circumstances, the only way to Britain might in fact be coming over to pillage it. Paperwork in this situation is obviously not necessary, as any sharp edged weapon gets the message across.

Information for Business Visitors

Red tape

Traders are most likely to encounter paperwork in two environments; on arrival at their port of call, and in contract work with the authorities.

The function of the former is likely to be to determine the level of taxation, if any, you are due to pay (see below in our section on Render unto Caesar), though some checks might be made on leaving to determine whether any fugitives are on the boat. When selling or buying goods from the authorities, such as buying state-mined lead ingots, or selling meat to legionary provisioners, the key point to remember is that there is a record chain that is being maintained to help plan for the bigger picture. A legionary commander, after all, needs to be sure that his outposts are getting the grain they need stockpiled so they can be fed through the winter. This also means that the books can be crosschecked, and embezzlement spotted.

It is possible that you might encounter a crooked dealer who will send more trade your way if you supply him with material or money 'off the books'. Note that even if instigated by the official, this is bribery and is harshly punished. To avoid getting into a situation where you are forced to choose between such a course or effectively losing a contract, we recommend you take a trading partner in there with you, such as an escort from your ship, to act as an eye witness. This may also help if any genuine misunderstandings arise from prices agreed in a foreign language. Again, see our section on counting in roman numerals: you may find it useful to take with you a small wax and wood notebook to agree (and preferably seal) the deal for later reference. Once agreed, however, you are contractually bound, and the authorities will look badly at you if you fail to keep your end of the arrangement.

Happily, red tape is less of an issue than you will find when traveling in the low season, particularly in the east, when various inventive new ways are being created to find money from citizens doing their daily business. But be prepared to accept difficulties and delays during times of social unrest.

Collegia

An institution you may come across, particularly if conducting business in Roman territory, is the collegium. These are officially recognised guilds under law, and are made up of members of just about any profession you can think of. At times, they are considered an unruly influence and might be curtailed.

Usefully, they may have rights to hold property in common, and so you might find they have assets such as meeting places or storage sheds that could be rentable. Meetings take place on planned days, and dinners are also organised which may prove a convenient way of making new business contacts.

Local Government

Depending on when you come means finding the place run from different spots. Looking for the capital and for the highlights of civilisation means different things at different times.

The first capital is Camulodunum. This gets wrecked by Boudicca, and it then becomes Londinium.

In the early third century, the province of Britain is split into two. The more peaceful south (Britannia Inferior) keeps Londinium as its capital; the north, however, or Britannia Superior is now run from Eboracum. While it has more soldiers, it's the junior slot.

At the end of the third century, there is a period of major administrative reform. Diocletian formally splits the empire, handing over the west to a colleague. In 293, it's split again, with a senior partner (Augustus) and junior (Caesar) for each half. Britain and Gaul together form one of the four separate 'tetrachies'. When a tertarch dies, the survivor can replace him by appointing a successor from a position of strength and legitimacy. That's the theory at least: in practice it goes pear shaped.

It's around this time that Britain is split up again into four smaller provinces. Lindum is the chief city in the centre/east, Britannia Secunda; the west, Britannia Prima, comes under Corinium; and the north and the south east are now renamed Flavia Caesariensis and Maxima Caesariensis respectively. Coordination happens at a new level called the diocese, which you can also find in Londinium.

So now you know where to turn up to if you've been invited to bid for a contract at the governor's offices (because your first question will now automatically be: which governor?)

Render unto Caesar

Taxation in the provinces is the concern of the governor or governors.

Taxes raised on immoveables (such as property) and associated goods used to be the business of the publicani, or tax farmers. These men would bid for the right to raise taxes; in return for delivering that sum, they would then do the business of finding the money and a bit more for themselves. However, by the time of Roman Britain, this business had been mostly banned due to the corruption and extortion that the system fostered.

Now, a new general wealth tax, and a tax per head, were imposed. This gets increased under Diocletian, when the major financial crisis gets addressed by restoring the currency and sorting out the old tax system.

But these taxes were focused on land, which as an outsider you won't be touched by. Your main taxes will probably be a local sales tax,

35

which will mostly run perhaps at one in one hundred rate, and the portorium or import/export tax. Portoria can also be charged if you are using the public roads, which is another reason why it may be in your interest to use a port nearest to your end destination. Note again that except for certain luxuries, these should only be levied where you intend to sell items rather than if they are for your own personal use, so be sure to check your duty free allowance, and you may find yourself exempt completely if selling to the state. The rate charged will vary from around two to four per cent, except in periods of crisis where they could increase significantly.

Try to time your visit wisely. There is also a tax known as the chrysargyrum, which appears every five years and is a currency tax on trademen and merchants. You may find tax collectors quite keen on chasing this one up, and a lot of people equally keen on avoiding it. If you have goods intended purely for your own personal use, you should again be able to argue you are exempt. If only occasionally visiting, you might be able to duck the attentions of the local trading association as they round up their members if they have been charged with collecting dues. But if you are trading on any scale you should not in any event be incapable of finding the extra revenue, or indeed of finding a local man of influence to lean on the taxman. Pity the borderline hand-to-mouth handicraft traders who find it very difficult to stump up and have to resort to all kinds of terrible things to make ends meet.

You will further need to be wary of two risks, however.

The first is the bad emperor. Bad emperors spend money. They need money. They take money. Often they take money in ingenious ways, meaning you can't predict how they'll do it. If travelling at the time of a bad emperor, either bring a lot of money (to pay lots of taxes) or no money (to pretend you are a poor swamp-living barbarian). You might try to hide highly taxed goods underneath low value goods, but you may risk losing the lot if you get caught.

The second risk is local need. During times when the empire breaks down, it's possible, if you have food supplies that the local legionaries need, that you might be forced to hand them over in return for being bartered something else. That might not be to your taste, in which case the best thing you might do would be to point out that if given a better deal you might be minded to return again with needed goods. At least, as a non-local, you won't be forced into a position of forced servitude to grow food for life.

In this climate, you'll see a lot of people getting poorer quickly. It pays to hide wealth when others are out to seize it, and spotting the key leaders in a town who have the hidden wealth will become more of a challenge for you as you look for someone to deal with. You might also be treated with suspicion at first if you try to break into a small closed society, until it becomes clear you're there to do business.

Under Diocletian, be aware that there is a series of price reforms setting the maximum limit for a large range of goods. Breaking this, even for small items, brings the death penalty. A number of products simply disappear from the market place. The measures won't last, but be very cautious not to get caught even selling something trivial at above the legal rate, and don't expect there to be many bargains actually available as they will likely all be being hoarded.

It's also important to note that unlike in Rome, there is no free grain. Don't expect food hand outs if you run out of money.

So as you can see, with social breakdown come opportunities for traders as coveted items become rarer, but they come with risks attached too.

Travelling Safely

Driving

No tests are required before obtaining a cart and horse, but you will find it good practice to drive on the left, especially when passing.

Health and insurance

Health is your own concern, though begging is possible in dire straits.

There is no insurance, unless you join a trade guild. Here you chip in a small fee. When you die, your burial fees are covered. You may also be able to find takers for property insurance, to cover you against fire.

Medical care is much better than at home. The very best comes with imperial service over in Italy, but even a qualified surgeon will be miles ahead of the types you can find back home. Look for a medical practitioner who is attached or has served with the legions, preferably Greek if you are lucky. These are highly skilled and trained. A good surgeon can be spotted by the variety of tools he owns, which he may even wash before use. The range of skills is such that surgery on the eye is possible, so not everyone has to end up looking like Wotan if they have a slight difficulty.

A classic tome doctors refer to is that of Celsus, writing in the first century. Here are some handy hints that may save you a doctor's fee

- Consider your diet as well as what medication and surgery might achieve.
- Reflect on a sick person's symptoms. These include tiredness, thirst, temperature, alertness, hunger, eating habits, gluttony, mood, dryness or wetness to touch, strength of sinews, habit of illness, lifestyle, energy and so on. Use of these observations to spot similarities between illnesses is known as "Method", but it can be highly controversial.
- Townspeople and scholars get sick more easily.
- Avoid eating too much or too little food, and eat savouries and salads

before your meat course, preferably roasted or boiled.

• Exercise in moderation, stopping when you break into a sweat.

• In winter, eat more and drink less, but make it stronger wine. Eat a lot of bread, boiled meat, and few vegetables. A little dry meat is best for lunch. Move to roast meats in spring, and in summer more vegetables, diluted wine, and cold or cooling food. Eat more often but less of it.

• Avoid sweating and excessive exercise during a period of pestilence, and avoid indigestion, if necessary by cutting down on meals a little.

• Some say baldness can be cured by applying burnt papyrus. This is nonsense. To encourage growth, shave the area and rub in ink.

• To get rid of spots, mix gum resin, soda and vinegar. After several hours, wash it off and apply oil.

• If you have a friend with something stuck in his ear that won't come out, tie him down (bad ear downwards) on a plank with the ends unsupported, and hit the end where his feet are with a mallet. Obviously, avoid his feet. The jarring should shake his ear sufficiently.

• Inflated testicles are cured by letting blood from the ankle. Boiled honey and cumin are useful salves.

• If you encounter a woman having trouble in labour, this is relieved by her sneezing.

• If you've been in a fight and you are now looking at your lower intestines, check to see if they are intact. If they are punctured, you are a dead man already. You have a small chance with your larger intestines so sling them over your shoulder and go to a doctor to get them sewn up.

• A colleague who has been bashed on his head has for his part little hope if he is stupified, his mind wanders, or is paralysed. Other wounds that look very serious might still be repairable.

• Bleeding a patient should not be done on the young, old and pregnant. It needn't be done at a distant part of the body, since the blood from the injured place would still also be drawn round; a good place to bleed someone after a bad head wound is the arm. If there is danger with a simple cut, special cups of bronze or horn are used, containing burning lint, to draw and drain. This will suck out enough of the badness to aid recovery.

• Remember that vinegar, possibly with rose oil, is a good thing to apply after surgery or on a wound in conjunction with lint or whatever clean materials you have to hand.

However, try to remember that there are several different medical schools, so you can find two or more doctors disagreeing on the necessary cure. Even worse, some of the clinical names are uncommon or confusing so that sometimes poisons like red lead get put into a potion instead of Indian cinnabar so make sure the pharmacist knows what's on the prescription.

There are a number of household remedies people will be able to tell you about for lesser conditions, such as using olive oil dregs for mouth ulcers.

Note that some famous ancient Greeks, Herophilus and Erasistratus, practised surgery by looking at the insides of live criminals who had been condemned. If you want to start a fierce moral debate, consider that at the dinner table.

Magic
Sorcery as we have pointed out is frowned on. But everyone has little farmhouse tricks that have been passed down, Britons more than most.

You won't find many druids left in Roman Britain as the Romans killed them all. In the north and in Ireland you will find them helpful and friendly - unless you insult one of their gods when they will lay a powerful curse on you.

Here's one for treating a dislocation or fracture if you can't afford a doctor. Split a green reed several feet long in two. Have two men hold it against their hips. Begin to chant this nonsense latin: motas vaeta daries dardares astataries dissuunapiter, repeatedly until the two halves come together. Wave an iron knife over it. Take the reed and cut it on either side. Fasten it to the injury. Then every day repeat this chant – huat hauat huat ista pista sista dannabo dannaustra. Or possibly huat haut haut istaris tarsis ardannabou dannaustra.

Other beliefs include curing toothache by biting wood that's been struck by lightning, or curing fever by tying a rope from a crucifixion around the neck, then burying it in a deep hole or cave.

Probably best to stick with the legionary doctor if you can find one.

Epidemics

Occasionally, great plagues arrive and kill off huge numbers of people.These are terrible things that swiftly overwhelm the body and end up slaying millions. The standard response is on its appearance to panic, leave town immediately and travel as far away as you can, before you breathe in the bad vapours which you will obviously be leaving safely behind rather than taking with you.

The huge plague disasters are the Antonine Plague during the time of Antoninus Pius, and the Aurelian Plague in the mid third century. There are other more localised dangerous ones too, such as a vicious outbreak in Rome in AD65. It may also be worth recording the Plague of Justinian in your diary, which strikes in the sixth century and keeps coming back for more. Consider avoiding the empire or any major trade routes if news reaches you that the plague is on the move. You might have a one in three chance of not living through it, and it crosses the entire empire and beyond, taking even emperors with it.

Cleanliness is Next to Godliness

For a Roman, keeping clean is a serious business. A visitor might even mistake it for a ritual. It involves a routine, a building, a professional assistant, and the provision of a service that leaves the individual in a better frame of mind.

Bath houses are buildings that have been specially created to serve these congregations. In our lands, we may be used to a quick dunk in the sea, pond or stream after an unfortunate slip in the pig pen. Some of our more eccentric hairy-chinned brethren might even consider relaxing in winter with some heated water thanks to some fire-heated rocks. Only the Romans go the whole hog and turn bathing into a process maintained by professionals. It is an extraordinary experience. If you are offered the chance to visit one, take it. It can be a stress-relieving opportunity, but it's also one that if you are a trader you won't want to miss for work reasons, because a lot of business gets done in these communal settings.

So what happens when you visit the baths? The first thing to note is that there are separate entrances, and separate working sections. Do not, under any circumstances, attempt to enter the female section unless you are a woman.

Slaves are permitted inside, as attendants, but young children will likely be turned away.

An entry fee will be charged, but this is typically only a small coin, a fact that accounts for their popularity across all ranks of society rich and poor and their regular and perhaps daily use. Larger baths could fit several hundred people in one go. As these will be maintained by the state, you may find their use free.

Leave your clothing in the changing room on the shelf. Next to each partitioned section there will be a number. You'll need to remember this in order to find your clothing again, though you'll probably be able to spot and smell it a Roman mile off when you get back.

For much of your time in the baths you will be completely

naked. This is normal procedure. Do not be alarmed if your massive frame, bulging biceps, hairy chest and bright hair colour draws attention to yourself. Part of the fun of visiting a bath house is the opportunity to flaunt your imposing barbarian physique compared with the shorter wiry Romans. In areas which have been less assimilated, and where there is a limited military presence, you may find closer physical similarity with the natives. Your long shaggy mane and facial hair could well still set you apart so even then it's likely you will still be recognised as a foreigner and not bothered unduly.

It is considered uncouth to allow bodily functions to operate in this setting, and discretion should be used in case of urgent need.

Once you have left your clothes in the care of the attendants, proceed immediately to the palaestrum. This is the physical exercise area where you can work out and build up some sweat before you get all clean. We suggest watching what others do before you try your hand. There is a skill to discus throwing that requires you to rotate your upper body rather than lob the thing like a rock, and damages to any nearby statues may have to be paid for. Equally, although most things are permitted in wrestling, eye gauging is expressly forbidden, and biting is frowned upon. Even with these small restrictions, it can be a very dangerous game, with breaks, dislocations and even death possibly occurring. Make sure you know how serious your contender is going to be before starting any bout, and be sure to submit and accept any submission at the sensible point. There is no point being a hero and then having to be carried to your lodgings with a dislocated knee.

You can find out more in our section on sport. Note that northern barbarians have a noted reputation of being extremely energetic in the short term but with no long term endurance, so if bets are laid, go for a sprint rather than any long run of several laps round the colonnades.

After some exercise, it's time for the baths themselves. The process is done through a measured scheme designed to make the most of the Romans' ability to manage room heating. The baths are fired by a furnace and the hot air funnelled, just like in private houses, under the floors to the rooms where it is needed. The hot rooms are quite humid (note the choice of stucco as the decoration to cope).

First is the tepidarium. This is where you take a dip into warm water to ease open your pores. Once you are relaxed, step out of the pool. In a well-run bathhouse you may find the floor of the next room painfully hot, so put on some clogs from the stock available and progress into the hot room, or caldarium. The combination of steam and hot water should be sufficient to really get you clean. Next, you need to cool down. Leave your clogs with an attendant and move onto the frigidarium. The cold plunge bath is only meant for a quick dip so don't loiter (not that you'll want to).

In the larger baths, ask if there's a laconicum as well to break up this process. It'll probably be next to the caldarium because of the heating vents. This is the sweating room. With the closeness of the room and the heated brazier it can get very intense, so don't stay in too long. Alternatively, ask one of the attendants to change the aperture, since there's a ceiling disk that can be lowered.

Any bath house worth its salt will have a room set aside for you to clean up. Olive oil is the perfect thing to help the masseur knead your muscles, before scraping it off with a special tool called a strigil. You may find you need to bring your own oil or a substitute: check before your visit, and certainly make sure you're getting the budget oil as some of it goes for astronomical prices. If you get accosted by the verbal antics of someone shouting shrilly, it's probably the hair plucker advertising his services.

Now go back to your clothes, get dressed, and go back onto the street. It's really that easy. Note that if there's a clothing

place nearby, if you've been travelling a lot and you've not got a spare set with you, you might want to consider tipping an attendant to nip round to get them washed. With luck they'll have a decent clothes press and by the time you've finished your clothing will be clean and mostly dry.

The baths are often places for informal social chats but also some general business. You might spot some hangers-on chasing after some local bigwig trying to fish for a dinner invite straight afterwards.

You'll find bath houses in most urban settlements, and even possibly in some of the larger private residencies, particularly in the countryside. It might be that the owner has a gong that is hit when he's taking one, just to let everyone know. Keep an eye open during your travels for sites associated with holy springs, as the supply of fresh water may mean an associated bath house of quality. The two examples worth stopping off at are the baths of Aquae Sulis in the west, and Aquae Arnemetia in the district with the peaks in the north.

If this process is simply too much for you, the Romans do have showers (Sergius Orata invented them a half century before Caesar's invasion), though we have not spotted one locally.

While we are on the subject of water and cleanliness, it may be appropriate to mention the public lavatory. Of course, we all know where we are and what we do when out on the country trail. But in built up areas, although the streets can get a bit pongy the locals really do not like to see people left, right and centre defecating in the gutter. This is where the toilet comes in.

Consider a bench with a hole in it through which your surplus waste drops. The hole extends to the front of your seat so you can access your underparts while seated. This is achieved by means of a sponge on the end of a stick, which is used to clean your nether regions before replacing your garments. A hidden trough of water under the bench sweeps the detritus away, while allowing the attendant slave access to flowing water with which to clean the sponge afterwards.

This can be a communal experience. With several seating places arranged alongside each other for a number of people to go at once, after a heavy set of oatmeal you may find you have time on your hands to discuss work and travel plans with others sharing the facilities.

Urine is a useful commodity and you may find it collected for reuse to fix dyes by clothiers. If someone asks you about whether you are taking some, it might actually be a literal question.

Equally, in more ramshackle accommodation you will simply find you have to make do with some old pottery that needs emptying in the morning rather than enjoying the luxury of anything piped in or away, or spilling over into the road outside. The Romans are justly proud of their sewers, which they have had for five centuries before they first stepped foot on these islands, as the cloaca maxima (or the Great Sewer) in Rome itself testifies. Eboracum sports a fine set as befits its legionary presence. But that doesn't mean that the convenience has spread to every house or isolated farmstead. The basic rule is: make do and adapt, but respect the local residents and use the local facilities whenever you can. And be careful where you are dumping the pot out of the window in the morning.

Money

Unless you have travelled a very long way indeed, there's a good chance that you've seen a Roman coin before you arrive, even if it's just as jewellery. The fact that they are made of precious metal, worth something in itself, gives a coin a basic value even outside of the areas where it has an exact value compared with other coins.

That fixed rate might take getting some used to.

Up to the end of the third century, it runs like this;

1 denarius= 4 sestertii = 8 dupondii = 16 asses = 64 quadrantes

HS is an abbreviation for the sestertius. You'll typically trade in these in any quantity. HS followed by a number means a cost, such as HS D meaning 500 sesterces. Add a line above that numeral, in this case the D, and it means 500 thousand. Make sure you don't get them mixed up!

If you are trading in big figures, there are also 25 silver denarii to an aureus, a gold coin. The rest are coppery or bronze. If you're trading in small figures, there are also semi-as (at half value) which are a lot less common than they used to be.

Later on, additional coins are added. The antonianus is a silver coin worth 2 denarii, at least until the amount of silver started to be cut. This is replaced by Diocletian with the argentarius, who also replaces the sestertius with the follis. The aureus is swapped for the solidus,

A denarius showing the head of Emperor Marcus Aurelius. Photo: Rasiel Suarez.

with less gold in it, under Constantine. At the other extreme, the tiny and fiddly coins we call the minim by now make up the really small change, which you're bound to keep losing.

This can all be very intimidating. The easiest thing to do is to focus on one coin (the sestertius is a good one for traders, an as for daily shoppers) and work out value and costs from there.

Clipping and debasement

Where the traveller and trader needs to take care with all these currency issues is over what the coin actually is. Is it the value it has back home, because of the silver in it, or is it the value it has here because of what the emperor says it is supposed to be?

Or to put it another way: imagine if an official cuts a coin in two and tells you half a coin is now the same value as a full coin because 'it's official and everybody has the same rate'- that's no good when you go back home and everybody sees you have half the silver you brought back last time, is it?

There are therefore three tricks you need to watch out for. The first is clipping. This is the practice where people who have coins cut the edges off to steal a bit of the silver from them before passing them on. This is illegal. You are quite within your rights not to accept coins from private individuals that you think have been clipped, and it is recommended that you use weighing scales to check coins that don't look rounded. It's unusual until the fourth century, and becomes more common when tax collectors become rarer to spot it. Punishment if caught doing it is harsh. If an official tells you the clipped money has just been ordered officially though, there is not a lot you can do about it as everyone is in the same boat.

Debasement is another, less visible risk. This is where the precious metals in coins are mixed with base metals, so the actual value is reduced. You'll find over time this keeps happening until it reaches a point of absurdity and coins lose all real value, and that now and again an emperor such as Aurelian will set the old standards straight again during a brief moment of peace. Then it will start again under an emperor who needs to find money in a hurry, which he does by taking it from the coins and making more, but less valuable, coins. Each coin is now worth less, meaning prices go up as shopkeepers demand more coins for their goods. This process is known as inflation. We barbarians only see it when goods are scarce because of war and famine, but prices drop again when things get better: this is not the case with Roman currency, for it is as if they have replaced overnight all their boars with twice as many little hogs.

Coins are struck in imperial mints. Watch out for those that aren't but look like they have been cast in moulds. A poor quality coin may be a fraud, made with even less valuable metal than the official ones. You can spot these counterfeits by them being considerably underweight. But also check the images – they are often badly defined for high value coins, and too crisp for the low ones, given the relative amount of wear and tear each should have.

Unfortunately that's not the end of it. Currency generally may be a bit of an issue for you in the import-export business. Nobody uses the gold coinage much except for high value, high bulk sales, so you should be alright at the ports. But there's very little silver, and while there's a fair amount of bronze floating around a lot of it is 'unofficial' local coinage that's been minted by the governor to get things done and paid. When silver does finally circulate a lot in the Mid Season, it's been massively debased, and by the end of the Low Season it's clipped away until barely the head of the portrait on the coin remains.

So overall, we advise you to do your daily transactions in the local coins, or swap goods of equal value, and take only the higher value coins with you if travelling on to another Roman province to avoid potential later difficulties. The basic lesson is to check the coins you deal in, especially in periods where the emperor is having major financial difficulties, and if the people are looking badly overtaxed. With really bad coins, you might even see it rub off showing a strange colour. If in doubt, always go back to your roots: barter.

Banks

If you run into financial difficulties, transactions can be done with the help of an argentarius. These are private bankers, found in private shops in the major towns. You'll probably first encounter one if you need to change currency. If you have foreign currency, these can be exchanged for a fee. Alternatively, if you have arrived with a large sum of money, this can be deposited with the argentarius for safekeeping. Since you are effectively giving him a loan, you should be able to obtain a profit yourself for this. You may be able to obtain from him a bill of credit, meaning that the sum might be drawn from another argentarius or used as a bill of sale, in either case saving you the difficulty and perhaps danger of carting sums of silver around the countryside. Argentarii also act as middlemen in public auctions, so you might find yourself dealing with one if buying a job lot of used military carts, for instance.

The Romans have a system called borrowing. This is a business transaction alien to us. Avoid taking out loans where possible, as fees may be high, and you might be expected to surrender a surety to ensure you don't sail away (such as your boat). On the other hand, they will check coins are legal tender, and so are a useful source of advice on debasement rates and clippings.

Ensure that all arrangements are logged in his official books, and aim for the larger and more reputable professionals in their line of business.

Working Out an Itinerary

Time

The Romans take the measurement of time very seriously, and getting to grips with it when working out a route for a series of trips may save you problems in the long run.

Time is marked in hours, starting from sunrise. Some take the trouble to measure time even during the night time, so that guard watches may be shared when the sun is not even shining. Ways of telling the time include the sun dial: it perhaps says something of the bloody minded Roman psyche that the first state sundial in Rome was set up incorrectly and it took them 99 years to add a correct one next to it. You can also use marked candles, and water clocks that mark the passage of time by the steady rate at which water leaks – handy when it's cloudy.

Individual days are distinguished and individually named as part of the measurement known as a week, and this is particularly important for those religions that worship on a set day. However, for your purposes it is more useful to understand the complicated way Romans follow months.

There are twelve, with a varied number of days in each. These are ianuarius (29), februarius (28, or fewer), martius (31), aprilis (29), maius (31), iunius (29), iulius (31), augustus (29), september (29), october (31), november (29), december (29). In an intercalary year, a special month of 27 days was added after February ,and February itself lost several days as required, since the calender year doesn't keep up with the movement of the sun over a year. Confused? That's just the start of it.

The first day of the month is called the Kalends. If someone says something will happen "on the Greek Kalends", don't check your diary: he means it will never happen, as there is no Kalends in the Greek calendar.

Now, the rest is more complicated. Remember this doggerel

and it will help you out: "On March, July, October and May, the Nones fall on the seventh day." In every other month, they fall two days earlier, that is to say on the fifth.

The Ides fall eight days later. That means on the thirteenth for eight of the months, and on the fifteenth for the four we just mentioned.

Now, if something happens not on those dates, you count back. If you tell someone to watch out for the Ides of March then they can expect trouble on 15th March. If a bit of bother was coming a day earlier on the 14th, then it would be I Id Mar (for one day before the Ides of March). If it were coming instead a day later, on 16th March, then you'd have to count back from the first day of the next month – with 31 days in March, that means xvi kal apr, or on the sixteenth days before the kalends of April.

Yes it's tricky: you might find it easier to say you'll meet again in five says time and have done with it.

Happily, past years are easier to talk about because the trend is to refer to the time when so-and-so was consul. The problem these days unfortunately is that you get several people holding the consulship in a given year, and sometimes (especially the emperors) on a number of occasions. In these situations, you'll hear it said that something happened in such a month on the third time that such a person was consul. Alternatively, count on from the year of the founding of the city of Rome, ab urbe condita, or AUC – thus Julius Caesar is murdered in 710 AUC.

Public holidays and festivals

Feriae are public holidays, many associated with a god. There are a lot of them, adding up to perhaps one day in three across the whole year, though you might find less 'towny' areas far less inclined to give up good plough time. You'll find business broadly suspended during the important ones, including slave work, and may find it prudent to plan your shopping

Playing dice is a popular game on Saturnalia, but watch out for cheats and keep you axe handy.

with this in mind. You might find though some work ongoing in areas deemed essential to safety and daily life, and you won't expect in this climate to see city dwellers decamp to the countryside for as long as they do in sultry Rome.

The key feriae are as follows. Note that given many of them are traditional Roman ones, you may find them most loyally celebrated amongst more recent immigrants from the peninsular, but some such as the Lupercalia (which involves people running around Rome pretending to be wolves) you'll have to go to see in the original.

We're all going on a summer holiday...

1 January: **Juvenalia**. Imperial games.

17 February: **Quirinalia**. Recalls the disappearance of Romulus.

19 February: **Charistia**. A family event for getting people back together again.

23 February: **Terminalia**. Honours the god of boundaries, including the boundaries of the Roman Empire.

24 February: **Fugalia**. Recalls the flight of the king before the Republic.

1 March: **Matronalia**. Giving of presents to beloved.

March: **Equiria**. Horse racing.

16 March: **Liberalia**. A disappointing version of the Bacchannalia, which

53

was far racier and got banned in old Rome. Also a coming of age ceremony.

19 March: **Quinquatrus**. Associated with Minerva.

25 March: festival to Cybele, and also a celebration of the equinox. General happiness.

Early April: **Cerealia**. Some women in white run around with torches. Not top entertainment unless you are a pyromaniac.

21 April: **Palilia**. Shepherd festival.

25 April: **Robigalia**. Wards off the evil god of mildew.

28 April – 2 May: Floralia. An Italian spring festival involving drinking and cavorting.

May: **Lemuralia**. Festivals to the dead. Throw some black beans over your shoulder to keep the dead away.

26 May: **ludi Apollinares**. Games with sacrifices.

11 June: **Matralia**. Honours the matres matutae.

21 August: **Consualia**. Horse and chariot races. Note that these animals get the day off, so limit your travelling.

11 October: **Meditrinalia**. Toasting new wine.

12 October: **Augustalia**. Only celebrated every fifth year, this festival recalls the birth of Augustus, the founder of the imperial system.

17 December: **Saturnalia** begins. At one stage, formed part of a wild cult festival. Now its a time of wild partying, to the extent that conventions are overturned, for instance with slaves playing at masters and everyone wearing the freedman's cap.

December: **Compitalia**. Veneration of the imperial lares. You might get some honey cakes out of it.

Uncertain timing: **Decennalia**. Ten years into an Emperor's reign. This is, sadly, infrequently held owing to problems qualifying. **Fornacalia**. Bakers' celebration, variable timings. Imperial weddings can also be celebrated: you can see people dancing in the street with garlands.

Individuals can celebrate their own particular events, such as a birthday, by taking the day off; and you might find the imperial birthday is added as a communal celebration across the empire. But you can see from the list, without going into how long each of these main festivals lasts for, that you may have to time your business carefully to catch your trading partner at the office.

Opening hours

Expect shops outside of festival days to be open during the hours of daylight, or until foodstuffs (bread in particular) sell out. Closing during lunch is more a Mediterranean practice but might happen if the owner is a smallholder with no slave to cover for him, or possibly in the height of summer. Shops in the vicinity of amphitheatres may adjust their opening hours accordingly.

Getting around

The wonder of Rome is its roads, and as we've seen you'll find a network across most of the populated areas. These are useful for wheeled carts in winter in particular. Don't expect the quality you'll find in Italy, but the facings will do, the drainage sections work, and going up hills you'll find you get some useful extra tread. They are also generally speaking well-maintained.

All roads lead to Rome? Not quite: there's water in the way. But you'll find direct links between all major urban centres, with useful mile stones regularly informing you as to the distance so you can work out how to stagger your journey.

Every few miles you will come across a mutatio or post house, which is where despatch riders can change their horses. Note for raiders: if you are on the rampage, that means word of your ship's dawn arrival at a watchtower would be in despatches fifty miles away by sunset even without lighting any beacons, and news of a major fleet arriving off the shore could be in Rome potentially in under a month.

Perhaps every five or so mutationes, every 25 Roman miles maybe, you'll find something bigger. This is the mansio. These are spaced far enough apart to suit a day's travel by road at a reasonable pace. They are large courtyarded buildings, with interior balconies. You may find facilities to affect repairs to your vehicles, such as a bent axle, or sort out issues with horse straps here.

Don't expect to be able to use the official service unless you have a special permit, and those are issued by the governor, and are often tightly restricted in number. Past-date permits will likely be rejected too. Some governors do issue these documents to close friends and relatives and the system is occasionally open to abuse, but it's better to assume that you won't be able to switch horses and travel at speed the next day unless you genuinely are on urgent business for the province. Then again, who wants to race on when you're on holiday?

There is also the option of coastal traffic by sea, which with fair weather conditions will obviously be quicker and more pleasant. In some places, for instance at Dubris, tall lighthouses have been built to show high fires out to sea so travellers can identify where they are, or tell where danger might be. Britain is easy to sail around, but given the size of the coastline a short road trip may end up quicker unless you have a lot of baggage or trade goods with you.

Accommodation

Where to stay during your visit is less of an issue than you might think. If you are on a budget, then camping just off the road side is perfectly acceptable, though depending on where you are visiting and with what illicit intent, you may find it prudent to set a guard. On the road, overnight stays might be possible at mansiones, which can also supply meals and basic provisions.

If you can't use these buildings, even at a price, then chances are it's because there's an inn nearby you're supposed to use instead along with the plebs. Ask for the caupo who runs it. Advanced booking is not required. In a larger settlement you may have a choice from which to pick: go for the one with fewer bed bugs, and watch your valuables. Food and drink will be available on site though they may be little more than snacks or even bowls of healthy eating, depending on the latest imperial edict.

Those with contacts might want to consider dropping in at a villa. As a welcomed guest, a stay in one of these rural retreats can be a refreshing halt at the end of a day's journey, and a source of some wonderful fresh countryside products. In extremis, such as a sudden storm, you might be lucky and be put up for a night, even if it's just in an outbuilding, though do as a matter of courtesy offer to pay.

Don't, whatever you do, simply materialise on the doorstep blowing your horns and shouting rowdy drunken battle songs if all you are after is bed and breakfast. On the other hand, these places are very isolated and make excellent targets if plunder is your game. Set a perimeter guard to see if anyone runs off into the fields nearby to hide a pot of coins in a hole if you want to maximise your booty: it's a common trick that has left many a barbarian disappointed with his profit margins.

It's possible of course that, instead, you have come prepared and already made preparations to rent a villa. Let's introduce you to how it'll look so you'll know your way around.

The Roman villa has become increasingly impressive in recent years. It was only in the time of the Emperor Augustus that a major fashion change took place that has had impressive results. Studius it was who first introduced artwork onto its walls, painting scenes of coasts, woods, landscapes and all manner of charming scenes. More than that, they have people in them going about their daily business, fishing, driving beast of burden, or even manhandling women.

It's a craze that has since caught on in all the best houses, and has proved to be eminently affordable across the empire (even if the quality varies massively). So as you go in, check to see in the entrance way if there are any portraits painted there. A well-adorned reception is a clear pointer already as to how sumptuous the rest of the house is going to be.

Enter via the vestibulum, the partly enclosed space that may be in front of the front door.

Key to understanding the house is the atrium, the central space leading off to other rooms. This is the heart of the building. If you spot an impluvium, or rainwater pool, in the middle of it, you have a design flaw as an architect fresh over from Italy's made it, and he doesn't know what winter is going to be like with a gaping hole in the ceiling. You may spot the sacellum or household shrine just off it. Opposite the entrance, you may find a tablinum, which is the room you'll do business in and store the paperwork. A really posh building might mimic a government building and have an exedra, a room fronting a little enclave where people could sit round and discuss things on a semicircular bench. The oecus is a large room sometimes used for banquets, though the dining room proper is the triclinium. Hopefully these won't be too far from the cucina or kitchens to make serving hot food a nuisance. If you're after the wine store, look for the apotheca.

The cubiculum is the bedroom, and you may find guests and their wives expecting to be put up separately.

The solarium is your best bet on a cold day, since that's the room that best catches the sun. Otherwise, you may have an agreeable garden, or viridarium, in which case make use of the portico when the weather is inclement. Larger houses, particularly those built up over some time, may have wings effectively forming a courtyard. There are also outhouses you can wander over and have a look at. If there's no door, it's probably the tomb of a former owner. If it looks like a shed with barely any walls, it's a pergula, and you'll find similar constructions being used in the city as stalls by artists selling their wares.

If you find a cylinder with holes at the bottom allowing grain or nuts to tumble out into little trays, don't nibble on them as it's not a snack store for you. They are bird feeders.

Food and Drink

Food

What good would life at the summit of civilisation be if there weren't things for the Romans to enjoy? Food comes near the top, and you'll find the variety astonishing to start with. If you can salt it, dry it, pickle it, spice it, or otherwise preserve it, catch it or grow it locally or at least within a few days road trip away, then chances are (for a price) you can eat it.

You might discover tracking down eateries that offer up dishes of the celebrated roast flamingos and candied dormice of decadent Italy a tall order all the same.

Still, that leaves you with quite a range.

Included in the list of game are goats, deer, boar, and hare. Pork and beef are popular, including parts of the head and trotters, as is chicken.

Bread is made from a variety of types of grain, such as millet and barley as well as wheat, and may be unleavened, that is to say it is flat as it has not risen. Sieves made of horsehair are a gallic way of sifting the flour.

A typical meal involves sitting at a table, so you should fit in well there. Lying about on sofas is confined to formal dinners.
Photo: Laura Haines

All manner of birds can go in the pot. The large walking birds are considered stronger foodstuffs than the others, so a thrush for instance is considered a light snack.

With respect to sea food, fish - unsalted or salted whole - are eaten in Roman lands. These can include for example mackerel, bream and bass, though fish living in rocky areas are considered less nutritious. Shellfish are very popular. The Romans introduced the technique of cultivating oysters into Europe, and they can be found transported into the very hinterland of Britannia. Make sure of course that it neither smells off, nor has refused to open if boiled. In certain parts you might find a readiness to eat whale and other sea monsters if they wash up to shore: the cooks certainly have their recipes. Lobster and octopus are harder to come by!

Fish guts are also allowed to decompose to create a strong, pungent (and probably for you, sickening) sauce called garum. It's expensive as the real stuff has to be imported – the stuff on the table may well have come from Spain. It's not only cost which should discourage you from going crazy with it on your plate: it's also prescribed as a laxative.

Honey and cheese are popular accompaniments, for instance in special strong pastries made of grain and lard.

For fruits and similar growing things, try the cucumber, beans, peas, turnips, onions, garlic, parsnips, beet, cabbage, lettuce, or asparagus. The olives considered best are the darker green, least ripe type, lightly and freshly pressed, and brought over from Italy. Then on stalks you can find grapes, nuts, and dates. Figs have to be imported from Egypt if you want to try them, so won't be cheap.

Snails you might want to avoid. Go for an egg, hard boiled or runny as you prefer. Raw egg is good for you. Some Romans even build special huts for doves to live in, in order to farm them.

Food preparation is a key component, and they have professional food preparers as well as small shops selling quick sit down or take away snacks. You can hear these stalls, called cauponae, before you spot them thanks to their attendants screaming out for business. Servings are taken from urns called dolia. Stewed food is considered better than salted, fresh meat over preserved, fat over lean, roasted rather than boiled. Salt and pepper are possible condiments.

If cooking for yourself and you find yourself looking for German butter, you mean here to look for the olive oil. The best is said to come from Campania in Italy, the area around Naples, though they say that too of its fish and shellfish.

If you have a dicky stomach and can't face anything too heavy, plump for gruel or a nice soft cheese, maybe with some spring lettuce and a nice piece of liver. Keep off the asparagus, leek, cress, mustard, pickled fish, kidneys, or large fish from muddy rivers. If you are really bad, what are best for you are lean meats, cherries, mulberries, certain pears, round apples, pomegranites, white olives preserved in salt water or vinegar or very well ripened black olives.

Fatty and sweet foods are renowned for causing flatulence. So too is stewed food, dairy products and most root vegetables. Onions, preserved raisins and sea urchins are a risk. You can limit your embarrassment by eating fennel.

If you have had a long trek but are having difficulty sleeping, then try poppies, lettuce and leeks.

Many of these food stuffs have been introduced to the province only thanks to the Romans, and in particular passed on discoveries made during their their wars in the Greek East in the century before the Invasion. Apricots, for instance, and cherries were two. Others the Romans brought with them were an interest in walnuts and chestnuts, better apples, and in farming chickens. Overall, they've come a long way from when the early Greeks chastised the simple farmers with the name of pultiphagi – 'porridge eaters'!

You are a long way from where they grow sugar and rice, or can find sunshine coloured fruit on trees, so be prepared for disappointment on these scores. Alexander the Great may have tasted bananas in India, but you won't here. You'll have to pay if you want Arabian or Ethiopian ginger, or peppers from the distant Caucusus (though some are grown in Italy). Arabian sugar is used only in medicine.

Some strange travelers lost from far over the broad seas might in vain look for these specialities;

- brown sweet tree nuts
- drinking beans
- dried infusion leaves
- underground tubules
- wheat dough tubes
- red squishy fruits, ideal for throwing

and other marvels such as the smelly fume leaves, but such delicacies are simply not known in these parts, at least not yet.
During a huge repast, don't be alarmed if you see people leave the table to

It pays to be polite to the kitchen staff. British appetites tend to be small, but you need extra food for all that dashing about killing and plundering.
Photo: Laura Haines

throw up. This is, it is true, a terrible habit and of no sound merit. It is intended to make space for more eating, where taste is considered paramount over the purpose itself. If you find you should never have plumped for the dish of snails, do speedily head for a discrete corner to avoid embarrassment such actions are done with a modicum of decorum (note these words are Latin for a reason).

Drink

Visitors will not be disappointed with the choices on offer. Note that the Celts and not the Romans prefer beer over wine, so choose your company carefully depending on your wassailing mood.

Some drinks are made from grain. Beware of the strength of those that come in small quantities and in various hues of amber. These Celtic beverages are very strong on the head, but are considered very nutritious. You might also possibly encounter fermented milk, mead, boiled down must, or raisin wine.

Rain water is lighter than spring water, and then river water, well water, melted snow, lake water, and finally water from a marsh. Heavier water is thought harder to digest but has more goodness in it.

Wines of course come in various forms. The best vintages were in the consulship of Opimius, a hot and sunny year, but that was two centuries before the conquest and now it's little more than honey. Anician wine, a close second, was another two generations older. The best wines are still these days Italian, especially the celebrated Falernian, also famous as it happens for its pears. The Greek island of Naxos comes recommended. You might want to plump for a vintage one and possibly add some water. Here are our recommendations;

- Maronian, from Thrace - a dark bouquet, strong, full bodied, improves with age. Best mixed with honey or diluted with water.

63

- Pramnian, from Smyrna – still famous since Homeric times.
- Setian – an imperial favourite that's taking over from Caecuban.
- Alban (near Rome) – mostly sweet.
- Surrentum – sweet, healthy, thin, but flat and dull.
- Mamertine, from Messana – favoured by Julius Caesar.
- Pompeian – ages badly, best drunk within ten years. It generates a terrible hangover (we concur).
- Clazomenae – taken with a tiny bit of sea water.
- Mount Tmolus – very sweet, mixed with dry wine.

You can also go local and drink milk. But why would you? Wine is given even to beasts of burden. Experiment with retsina, mixed with resin, instead.

Liquids are stored in a variety of large containers called amphorae. Tip: pour into a drinking vessel rather than try to drink straight from the rim, as they are very heavy

Formal Dinners

Barbarians get nervous easily at formal dinners, what with the strange cutlery and the expectations of having to lie down to eat. It's very different from life as an auxiliary, with your cooking pot perched on the shared grid iron and just getting on with the cooking yourself. But in fact, if you are invited to a dinner, there's no reason to be concerned.

First, a word on the etiquette of greeting. You probably won't be expected to follow the custom, but among the upper classes a brief kiss is the tradition. Allow yourself to be shown to your seat. Arrangements are done by precedence, with the most important people nearer the host, so don't assume you are meant to just sit anywhere.

Do use the cutlery, if you can. Watch others to see how they do it. Knives are for cutting, not stabbing. Spoons are for cutting and scooping: the tiny ones are for eating eggs, shellfish and snails. No-one will probably be too upset if you use your hands for chunkier dishes, given your background. Slaves will be around to help if things go badly wrong.

Any ladle with holes in it is probably a wine strainer, used when the wine's been heated and spices added. Leave that to the servants to play with, but do flavour your plate with seasoning from the salt cellars, or the small condiment pots.

Food will be served in several courses. First there is the gustatio, or starter course to get the taste buds going. Then there is the prima mensa, or main course. It's rounded off with the secunda mensa, or desert. Posh bashes will have many additional courses as sub sets of these, so leave space if you know it's an all-nighter.

You may find you don't need to recline. True, fully-signed up Romans do have a habit of stretching out on their couches, placed three quarters around a central table so that three diners can be within arms-reach of the food at any one time. But that's the men. You might find women and children will be eating sitting up, and you can probably get away with joining them if you can bear a couple of jokes at the outset.

The dining room is not the place for talking business though, and it's a faux pas to attempt it. This is a time of relaxing, as you'll find confirmed when the musicians and performers later appear. Check when you enter to see if it's an all-male

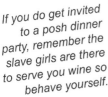

If you do get invited to a posh dinner party, remember the slave girls are there to serve you wine so behave yourself.

65

gathering, and if hip wiggling dancers from Gades are on the menu. That might determine how interesting the entertainment is going to be like.

There are some other social mishaps that can be readily avoided. Break egg and snail shells after eating their contents, to avoid jinxing. Say 'bless you' when someone sneezes. And note that leaving a table is bad form as an even number of diners brings bad luck.

You'll need to bring a napkin. This can be used at the end of the dining to take away some leftovers, though it's advisable not to help yourself until you've seen a number of other people doing it first so as not to get a reputation for being there just for the food. For the same reason, go for a mix of food rather than just aim for triple portions of the rare stuff. Leave anything that's dropped on the floor for the dogs.

Of course, it might be that you are dining in rather less celebrated company. In these circumstances, you'll probably be tucking into a mix of home grown vegetables and salad things, possibly with some cheese and vinegar. Unless you're in the countryside where livestock's to hand, don't count on there being meat. You may get some porridge or something fishy, plus a fresh homemade loaf. Grin and bear it – you're with ordinary folk now.

A famous Roman writer by the name of Horace once wrote a satire comparing these two ways of living, in a story of a country mouse and a city mouse. The city mouse visits his rural friend but disdains the basic fare and encourages him to join him back in the city. But their fantastic feast is interrupted by the mansion's residents and the arrival of the dogs. The country mouse decides his little hole in the forest is enough for him. You might find as you watch the Roman ways of living that wealth brings luxury, but stresses and dangers of its own.

Style and Fashion

What to wear

You may find clothing takes some getting used to. While you will not be expected to wear a toga, these curious articles are worth keeping an eye open for as their appearance indicates an assimilated individual of some standing, or perhaps even someone who has come from the heart of the empire. They are very old-style statements, intended for formal public display. A toga consists of a large strip of cloth, half-oval in shape. One end is wrapped tightly around the waist, then the other is flung over the shoulder and wrapped around the arm. Loose change may be kept in the folds. Traditionally, purple bands on their toga indicate someone has rank, thick for a senator and thinner for a mere 'knight', and a pure white toga (candida) means that someone is running for office: hence a candidate. Simple tunics are more likely, however. More than one layer might be worn in these climes. Stick with what you know and don't try wearing a toga: someone might think you are trying to impersonate a full Roman citizen with all the legal rights that go with it.

You are far more likely to see more traditional forms of clothing the further away you go from the towns. Bracchae, or breeches, have even become popular amongst the legionaries posted on the northern defences – quite understandably, soldiers have noticed that their traditional uniforms lack the leggings needed to protect them from windy blasts, and they do not like it up them. You might also come across some gloves if you know where to look.

You will probably find your usual items of clothing are not the high point of attire. While in our lands you can often see heavy woollen clothes marked with dyed bands, lighter cloths may be more the rage in urban areas. Don't expect to see much of the fabled silks. Although they have been known in Rome itself since before the conquest, the cost is massive, and only

Roman style clothing for women is very practical given the climate of Britain. Photo: Laura Haines

the rich and powerful can afford it in the third century. By the Low Season, however, a huge craze has pushed the price down so that even more common folk can begin to afford it, though so much gold is leaving the Empire that attempts are made to bring the level of trade down, so you may still be lucky and be able to pick up locally some exquisite clothing fit for a barbarian chieftain's wife, though don't expect to pick up any bargains. The best is from China, but it's also made in Assyria, and on the Greek island of Kos. Persian islands supply a sort of 'wool' called cotton.

Cloaks remain a popular fashion accessory, and indeed there are several different types from which to choose, including some versions with hoods. The British one, the byrrhus britannicus, provides best protection and comes in quality wool, reflected in its price. In many cases, they are kept on by their top corners being tied together by means of a brooch. Unlike our own barbarian brooches, these tend to be relatively plain rather than inlaid with wondrous precious stones. They may still, however, be finely made, and traders should take note that their form may vary as preferences change over time, the fistula design of one year being seen as quite 'yesterday' by the time of his next visit if a significant gap has intervened.

Travellers in later seasons will note an increasing tendency to wear sumptuous and brightly coloured garb and conspicuous wealth. This helps identifying both ideas for presents, and whom to rob. Anyone announcing for instance that they are always clothed in expensive hedgehog skin, for example, is asking for trouble.

Women's Clothing

A discerning barbarian will obviously not be wearing women's clothing. However, on the off chance that a gift is being considered of native wear as a present for the return home, or a disguise is very urgently needed, a few words may be in order.

The stola is the long tunic which reaches down to the ankle, thus longer than a man's tunic. This can be matched with a light cloak, and accompanied by jewellery such as a necklace, bracelet of earrings.

A bulla is a large pendant worn by children or unmarried young women.

Underwear

Don't be spooked if you encounter garments worn under these clothes. Barbarians might like to enjoy free

range access, and in the olden days this was the way things used to be under the toga, but nowadays this is often considered uncivilised

You won't get to see women's underwear much, but the dancing girl shows are an exception.

in these parts. The subligaculum acts as a pair of tiny legless pantaloons, and you may find people wearing it while exercising at the baths. Women may also bind their tops with a strip of cloth. If you are likely to be getting out and about on a chilly day, or doing a lot of chasing victims through brambles, invest in a subligaculum. You'll feel the difference. You can get them in cloth or leather.

Washing your clothes

In polite society, there's no reason to maintain that mud-spattered slightly suspiciously bloody look. When in town, take the opportunity to get your clothes cleaned (and wear a spare set when you do). Wondered what happens to the urine that's gathered at public lavatories on street corners? It's used as part of the washing process. Your clothes will return properly aired and stretched with a magical freshness. Best not to send your woollens though as they may shrink.

Footwear

Take your pick. You can go for a sort of soft leather boot. It you are a bit more hard core, or stepping in mud a lot, you could try sandals. These are the old legionary favourite, and even gave their name to an emperor (Caligula, named after the little boots he wore as a child when paraded in toddler soldier uniform). The army types have studs on which give good grip but also mean you can hear the legion crunching on hard surfaces from miles off. Later soldiers prefer boots called socci, increasingly also with some thin padding. Poor people may wear clogs.

Note in particular that in some cases, the right and left footwear may actually be shaped for the foot, so if you are having difficulty walking, try swapping them over. We recommend if you need to buy a replacement set during your visit, showing your foot to a boot maker and getting something barbarian size specially made. Grabbing an issued pair off a dead legionary may leave you with both aching big feet, and some explaining to do if you encounter a patrol on a later visit.

Hair today...

Hair styles change over time. Don't get caught out; get coiffeured.

It starts off short but a little moppy at the time of the Conquest. Curls and sideburns are in at the time of Nero. A maintained greater abundance of hair accompanies the beard rage in the second century. The slightly 'boxer' look is in for much of the third century.Pudding bowl haircuts are much more the rage in the fourth century.

Women's hairstyles adapt even more regularly. In urban centres, you'll quite possibly see hair styled, unless at certain events such as in mourning. Hair early on is often plaited and worn behind. Hair nets are the vogue when Nero's on the throne. By the second century you have mad curling going on making the hair gather up front like a dandelion, or rising to peculiar peaks looking from a distance almost like a helmet. These may be wigs so don't expect these ladies to be stopping to pick up anything you might have dropped: in fact, give them a hand if they do.

Blond is definitely the new black! You'll soon realise that there are a lot of dark haired Roman types in Britain, and auburn haired Celtic types, but fair hair is rare. Best for you, it's all the rage amongst Roman women. If you run out of money, consider selling off your golden locks to a wig maker and you might find yourself literally with a head for money.

Beards styles also will alter. The old style Celtic look might include a stylish moustache, but less chance of anything on the chin. The Romans were big on shaggy beards in the old days, and Cato the Censor was famous for his. Then as beards were seen as a bit too 'unsophis', clean cut comes in - though at the time of Caesar's visit, in social circles in Rome you could see people wearing what old fuddy duddies called 'barbunculi', or silly little beards.

It's a phase that doesn't really last, particularly in military circles. However, beards come back in in the second century AD when fairly substantial ones start to be worn by the emperors themselves. In the third century, you can see shorter beards again, and in the fourth after Constantine they tend to disappear once more. So you can tell a lot about the timings of when you are in Britain from what beards are up to. It might be just a coincidence but you'll feel at home in Rome's golden age, and beardedly out of place when they start to have major issues with you. Maybe it's an identity thing, or perhaps just the way of fashions.

Perfume

This Persian invention does take on in Britain. It is supplied in small slender bottles, at huge cost. Balsam, for instance, is grown in two small gardens in Jerusalem. Then, come the Jewish Revolt the Romans just manage to save the species by rescuing the last bush from destruction by the rebels. Many other ingredients have to come from further afield.

Perfumes are even used to anoint military standards, and some people strangely add it to their drinks. A dried version is talcum powder.

Assuming you can transport the containers safely, this makes for a high value, easily transportable, item or valued gift.

Information Technology

Communications

The official messaging service involves couriers, but don't expect to be able to use it. Instead. You'll have to rely on a slave (if you can spare one) or the goodness of strangers heading off in the right direction to carry any of your letters.

Providing you are not in a hurry, the chances are your correspondence may arrive. Don't, under any circumstances, post valuables, breakables or perishables, or things that are heavier than they looked when the traveller initially agreed to carry them on.

The Media

Over in Rome, the official news gets written up on special white boards, or acta diurna. But news travels slowly so what is daily (diurnus) in the capital quickly gets out of date over here.

Enter the praeco, or herald. His job is to make public service announcements, and you may even be able to hire him out. If it's a question of lost and found, an auction that needs advertising, summonsing for a trial, or an official statement such as indicating that the senate had passed some new law, then he's the man to listen to.

As for everything else, well that's just gossip.

Pastimes

Games

Dice games are popular. Note that they may be associated with gambling: make sure you aren't playing for money you can't afford to lose before you begin. It also might be illegal, and a good fraudster will have a set of loaded dice waiting for an out-of-towner to turn up: your best bet is just to stay clear.

You might also find scratched onto seats and handy tiles the boards for various types of counter games, such as a wheel of eight spaces with another one in the centre, where the objective is to get three in a row. These are quite straightforward to learn and are a good way of breaking the ice.

If you fancy something a little more physical, there are a variety of ball games that you can try out involving foot work or throwing things around. Balls might be colourful and stripey, or even just an inflated animal skin. Make sure you are not throwing an exercise ball, which is heavy and meant for flexing your muscles rather than expecting any lightweight Roman child to catch.

Sport

For many Romans, physical entertainment is something you watch others do, especially if it involves danger. There's nothing more perilous than a trip to the amphitheatre, especially if you're the star attraction.

The biggest of these awesome constructions are all to be found in Italy. Of course, there's the Flavian amphitheatre in Rome, begun by Vespasian near the colossal statue of Nero (whence its name of Colosseum). Next is the amphitheatre of Capua, built only a couple of hundred yards from the site of the predecessor known to Spartacus. Even the third biggest, at Puteoli in the Bay of Naples, was considered grand enough for an Emperor to take a Parthian Prince to show off Roman culture (he responded by impressing the crowd with some amazing archery from the grandstand).

You won't find anything quite so grand in Britain. But no matter: you're there for the entertainment not the architecture.

Happily laws have tightened since the great disaster at Fidenae in the time of Tiberius, when a shoddy wooden amphitheatre collapsed killing thousands, so you should be safe – especially as chances are you're in an edifice built by capable legionaries. If you're in a town with an amphitheatre, and there are several across the island, it may well be that you're in an old garrison town. The legion brings Romanisation in its baggage.

So what can you expect in a show? Gladiators paired off in traditional duels, with individuals equipped in a standard way to offset the advantages and disadvantages of the other.

Gladiators fight according to very strict rules and have referees to make sure they don't cheat.

The murmillo has a hulking helmet, shield and a tiny sword, features common to the provocator though in style and appearance pleasantly distinct. The retiarus is the net man, with minimal armour but carrying a trident, allowing him range but little protection. His opponent is the secutor, who has a helmet, a shield and a short sword. Regular show attenders might also see some unusual experiments with new types of gladiator, such as ones dressed in so much armour they had a tough time even moving. As compensation for their opponents, these crupellarii are armed with what passes for a butter knife.

Death doesn't always follow. When one fighter has the other at his mercy, the crowd make an arm gesture to say whether they think the loser should be spared, and the host makes the decision. Gladiators are expensive commodities so not all fights are blood baths. Probably the grimmest will be those where criminals have been sent in to fight to the death, since the crowd really does expect blood and they are given nothing but the weapon. The winners of these matches fight each other until they all die, or try to flee and are burned. And they call us barbarians! One German, doomed to face the animals, decided to cheat the audience and choked himself to death using a toilet stick. Another condemned man stuck his neck in the wheel of the cart taking him to the show.

A decent show could last quite a while. Rather than risk the food sellers not making it round to your part of the seating, bring a snack. Also, some water would be a sensible precaution on a hot day, just in case the awnings that these buildings often are meant to have turn out not quite to cover your stretch of the seating.

The amphitheatre, and to a lesser extent the theatre, is a good way of telling a fellow's status. There's a special box for the magistrate, and the host of the games. The most important and wealthiest sit at the front and the poorer at the top. As a foreigner, your place will be at the back with the slaves: don't take this too hard as you'll still get a grandstand view. Try not to make too much of a nuisance with yourself if there are married women at the back behind you sheltering from the climate. In Britain these divides are less obvious than in Rome which is packed full of important people with clearly defined ranks, in the Senate and in the equestrian class of the well-to-do. But still, watch out you're not taking what's designated as a soldier's seat.

Under no circumstances leap into the arena to participate in the action.

Outdoor pursuits

Maybe watching other people do all the fighting and get all the fun is not your thing. In which case, why not consider going hunting? It's true that the deer aren't as impressive as those on the continent. Even so, Britain's sleek hunting dogs are world famous, and it would be a shame to miss out on the opportunity to put them to the test. They have a reputation for speed as well as a strong bite.

You can elect to chase a hare or something a little more dangerous (see our section on wildlife dangers), but remember if so to borrow a special hunting spear to bring with you. If you fancy trapping and an opportunity to make a bit of money on the side, it shouldn't be beyond your honed barbarian skills to hunt down a beaver if you have the spare time, and claim yourself a pelt along the way.

Check before you go as to what type of hunt it is, however. Many of the posher urbanised Romans have nets set up into which beaters drive the wild animals while they have a picnic, waiting to make the final kill. This is hardly the stuff legends are made of, and is barely much better than watching some condemned criminal run around an amphitheatre chasing a rabbit.

Alternatively, grab a special spear and go fishing instead. The cold streams of the north abound in salmon and trout.

Law and Disorder

Government

Back in Germany even where we have kings, we have more of a tradition of holding regular open councils, and everybody turning up with their weapons to discuss matters. Obviously, the most important people, often the oldest, get to speak first but the decision is collective, depending on whether everyone murmurs, wave our spears, or clash them on our shields.

The Roman Empire, however, is an authoritarian state. Everything is run by people appointed to run it. Some management posts, such as guilds, are elected. Some local management posts, such as someone running the day to day business to keep a town working, may be also. But do not confuse this with a true democracy such as the ancient Romans enjoyed. Remember that you need to appeal in your actions to the few rather than to the multitude, for that is seen as the act of a demagogue and a threat. Visitors serving in with the legions should pay particular notice of this rather than mark themselves out from the outset as a troublemaker. Forget the Senate: the army forms the last place of any democracy in the empire as the one place where numbers decide who the empire's leaders will be.

Crime

Pick pocketing can be a menace, and you may need to anticipate the threat even of someone cutting draw strings with a small blade and walking off with the whole purse. Similarly, ensure that if you leave valuables in your room while at a mansio, even though the entrance doors are in common sight it is wise to secure the door after you. Windows often have secure grilles on them, while the Romans have sturdy doors that bar by means of inserting a piece of metal called a key into a hole called a lock. On rotating the key, the door jams shut. Keep the key in a safe place, for instance in

78

your new underwear. Also remember that most locks are not complicated, and any lock is only as good as a weak door frame, and as bad as the lock picker.

While at a bath house, you might wish to consider tipping one of the slaves who watches the clothing shelves to encourage him to pay extra vigilance as these places can attract professional thieves. 2 denarii is the going rate in Diocletian's day.

While it will be obvious to everyone around you that you are a foreigner, if you present an appearance of knowing roughly what you are doing you should not attract excessive unwanted attention. Be wary all the same of fraudsters offering you a service, such as acting as a guide, at excessive rates paid for in advance.

If you get into a brawl that escalates, and you hit someone with something, quickly spit into your weapon hand. This shows instant contrition and reduces the resentment caused.

Travelling in rural areas can become an issue in the late third and fourth century when brigandage becomes more common. In Gaul and Spain these are called Bagaudae, in Syria for a brief while they prosper as the Maratocupreni, on the Danube they are the Scaramae. But essentially they are locals who have just had it up to here with all the taxes and imperial edicts and price rises that are crippling them. If you bump into a group of them, they might be more lenient towards you as you're not an agent of the emperor, in which case give them some bread and be on your way. Otherwise, you might be out of luck, you may fall into a hardened bunch and you've a fight on your hands. Go for the hungriest looking rascal first and make it count.

Legal matters
Romans are less fond than us in hanging traitors from trees, or smothering cowards and the vice-ridden in bogs. Decisions are made by professional judges, though we have once

witnessed a trial with a jury or body of locals of some standing, not unlike the body of a hundred that are appointed to assist in reaching decisions in trials back home.

Rome is a society built upon the rule of law, and there are professionals who exist to support either side in a dispute. Settlement is by an official of the state, based on argument in the context of established law.

Contracts, it is important to note, are considered binding rather than advisory, so if you attempt to defraud a local trader, you had better avoid visiting his town for quite a while or risk being sued.

If you break the law and end up in jail, you may hire a lawyer to argue your case (advisable, unless your Latin is good). This will cost you: there is no free service. There is no trial by combat, sadly.

Although you are not protected by the laws governing

Roman subjects, since you aren't one, you remain protected by basic laws that affect all peoples. This 'international law' is called the ius gentium. Happily, this means that certain property rights and commercial rights are basically protected, so no one can just walk up and try to confiscate your goods.

Roman lawyers wear the formal toga when in court. It is possibly the most ridiculous item of clothing ever invented, but you should get one as a souvenir to take back home for a laugh.

80

Note that men have more legal rights than women, particularly the father of a household. Bear this in mind when signing contracts. Women with several children can have more rights, however.

As a quirk, note that thanks to Constantine later visitors might encounter a change in the legal system, where for a short time either party might appeal to a bishop to try a case, and the local authorities would be required to enforce the decision. This system won't last and might give you some additional legal difficulties. But you might consider using it as a delaying tactic if the bishop is on holidays, or if you are having problems with a prolific temple builder of the old school.

Prostitution is legal in the Roman world. The establishment is called a lupernar, though you might find it also doubles as your inn.

Personal safety

The world is a dangerous place, what with all those cut throats, wild animals and barbarians out there. Don't go down dark alleys; don't flash your silver around the place, especially when drunk; and if waylaid out in the woods, get the opening blow in first.

Barbarians have a reputation for being insane killers. Make the most of it and anything less than a determined criminal gang may run away.

In towns do note though that there are officials whose job it is to police the streets. These are the vigiles, who also double as fire patrols. If you are causing trouble, you might expect to be arrested. On the other hand, if troubled in a town, you should consider using only appropriate force against your opponent. If you have been jostled in the street and you respond by beheading the miscreant, you might discover the vigiles consider the reaction disproportionate and excessive. In which case, run.

Vigiles do not constitute a major obstacle to a rampaging war band, you will be delighted to learn.

Volcanoes
There are no volcano issues in Britannia.

Treason
Visitors to the Roman Empire are unlikely to be embroiled in claims of treason. This is just as well, as the likely consequence would be imprisonment, torture, and horrible death. Happily, a number of factors reduce the threat of such a fate.

In the first instance, as foreign subjects, you are technically exempt since you can only properly speaking be treasonous to your own regulus or petty king. Since association with treachery is also likely to carry the death penalty, this is cold comfort.

Secondly, visitors to Britain are considerably removed from the imperial court and the heart of power. The likelihood of plotting taking place on the outskirts of the Empire is perceived to be lower, though it still does happen, particularly in areas of strong military presence. Being a barbarian rather than a Roman obviously however reduces your sway with traditional legionaries, who are less likely to follow troublemaking foreigners leading them into wars against their own kind. Being very foreign also means you have no imperial blood in you from any current or past claimant, and thus no 'look at me' status.

You may get away with rough jibes in taverns unless in the company of German auxiliaries. Batavians, or German mercenaries from where the Rhine reaches the northern sea, also have a reputation for loyalty so be wary of loose talk in their company. In Domitian's time in Rome itself though, soldiers dress in civilian clothing and start conversations criticising the emperor to see if you join in, at which point they arrest you.

A third feature in your favour is wealth. Much of the business about impeaching traitors is actually to do with greed. As a traveller, you will not be carrying insanely large amounts of money around with you. To be frank, and some readers ethnically are, what passes for a rich Roman worthy of being done over in this way is someone who owns a slice of Africa, or enough precious plate to build a trireme out of silver. A barbarian's purse and a few coins and trinkets is unlikely to attract malicious intent.

That said, when in polite company such as a dinner, do watch out for the delatores. The delator is the professional informer. You can generally spot them as they hover around conversations like flies drawn to honey, perched inquisitively, until people spot them and move off terrified. In company such as this, any word from yourself may be seen as confirmation of other allegations and it is best to hide behind language ignorance until they have left the room.

Delatores have appeared at many times, typically when an emperor is (i) mad (ii) bad (iii) financially broke. As a general rule of thumb, if visiting during a period when the Emperor insists on being referred to as a living god, always be guarded in what you say.

Examples of the sort of things that might land your associates in difficulty include;

- Wearing purple, the imperial colour, or having purple furniture
- Owning (and refusing to part with) valuable goods, such as Corinthian vases or tables made of citrus trees from Mount Atlas
- Suggesting things used to be better under the old emperor
- Being too closely related to the incumbent
- Having something eg a horse coincidentally carrying the same name as someone who's been executed
- Mentioning the Republic (even a 'good' Emperor like Vespasian would execute tiresome types like members of the 'Stoic Resistance' who incessantly kept extolling the old unfashionable systems of government, ie ones that excluded him)
- Ostentatious wealth (during an early cull in the civil wars before the

Empire, one proscribed individual on spotting his name on the hit list exclaimed that his gardens had undone him)
- A bad joke involving someone in power
- Saying innocently how marvellous it must be to live life as an emperor
- Investing in sharp cutlery

A terrible example takes place in the reign of Constantius, here in Britain itself. As a ruler, he has surrounded himself with flatterers, foremost amongst them a Spaniard by the name of Paulus. Be very wary as he turns up in Britain to sort out who had conspired with a former claimant for the crown. As soon as he's there, Paulus turns on anyone with any wealth. He imprisons freeborn citizens, even using handcuffs which Romans consider highly debasing, based on claims that are complete fabrications. Not for nothing is his nickname Catena, "the chain"! The acting governor, the heroic Martinus, repeatedly but powerlessly implores him to free the innocent, and on receiving no response threatens to retire. In response, Paulus threatens to add Martinus and a number of his officers to the list of people being sent to the Emperor.

This is too much for Paulus, who attacks him with his sword. Failing, he kills himself with his blade. The prisoners from Britain are dragged away in filth, to be tortured on the rack and by hooks. Many are proscribed, others are exiled, some face the block. Don't count on anyone being acquitted in this era.

Happily, not all emperors are inclined to the trend. After this very bad stretch, when the Emperor Julian came to the throne he quietly ended the practice, which still left a lot of bad blood when old informers turned up at social gatherings expecting to be treated as friends. On the other hand, when he was travelling through Cilicia a delator turned up and informed on a fellow townsman, telling tales on how he was making his own purple cloak. Instead of lopping off a head, Julian merely indicated that when he had finished dyeing the cloak, he would drop him off a pair of purple slippers too. The point was subtly made: the mad DIY clothier had been pushing his luck, but a wise ruler knew that it took more than a bit of inventive haberdashery to make a threat, and the delatores were out of business and should know that too. Or they might, like Paulus the Chain, end up being burnt alive.

Slavery and Classes

Slavery is everywhere in the known world, and the Roman Empire is no exception. You may even find some German slaves taken in war or exported across the border into Gaul.

From the moment you enter a house and see the doorman chained to the doorpost, to the worker you might see labouring in the fields in the rain, slavery is all around us. Unlike in our lands where slaves are rarer and they live almost as locals, their lot here varies massively, depending on whether they are expected to work the mines or instruct their owner's children in grammar. Some jobs can be quite cushy, like the nomenclator whose job is to remember people's names. Corporately owned, or part of the imperial estate, on the other hand, good treatment comes second to profit. That said it took an Emperor, Augustus, to overrule the cruel Vedius Pollio, who had a habit of throwing his slaves into a pit full of lamprey eels to be eaten alive. Yet where slaves are incorporated into a family they might even be treated as sort of part of it, even to the point of being buried together. Rented slaves on the other hand often get treated very badly indeed, since their temporary owner is trying to make most use of their services from the contract to make a profit.

The objective of many a slave is to buy his or her freedom (manumissio): a privilege and ambition so widespread as to be perhaps unique to this slave-owning society. This is probably just as well given the number of slaves knocking about, especially in Italy. The peculium is the money they are allowed to keep, or the property they are allowed to own. Small tips you might as a visitor offer for good service rendered might in fact be contributing to changing their lifestyle for the better. A freedman, or ex-slave, has more rights, and may indeed be taken on as an employee by their former owner. A freedman's son in turn becomes a free man, that is to say born free, and enjoying still more legal rights. Imperial freedmen can enjoy considerable power, so don't cross them. One of Nero's was so rich he not only put on a gladiatorial show, but had life-like portraits made of the combatants for the public walkways. Later on, the VIP set can include eunuchs. Try not to mock well-dressed beardless people with high pitched voices as they might have the ear of some very powerful people.

With the passage of time, the legal distinction between the haves and the have nots shifts from that of the slave class to one of money. The honestiores are the upper class, and the humiliores the lower class. If brought before a law court in the low season, try to make out that you are a better class of barbarian and be counted amongst the former, as the punishment is far more tolerable and involves less torture, crucifixion, being eaten by animals, and digging of mine shafts.

Free people can sometimes be mistaken for servants because of a system of patronage. Rich people can have an entourage of clients. As a patron, they look after their interests, and look good by having a number of fawning people around them. This is not to our tastes but it can mean that you have a friend in a higher place, or someone who can loan some money. When dining in proper Roman style with someone who is a patron, you might see the guests graded. It's a useful way for you as a newcomer to judge the relative importance of people you might be doing business with, watching one grapple with cheap wine while another has more expensive stuff but in small cups. One famous Roman bon viveur called Lucullus, who was fabulously rich, was tested by Cicero and Pompey dropping in on his mansion unexpectedly, not leaving him any chance to prepare for their arrival. He cheated by having a system, so that when he ordered dinner to be set up in a certain room the budget and menu was already known to the servants. These things are taken very seriously indeed.

The legal conditions affecting slaves do improve over time. Several large slave revolts first taught the Romans to fear them. If a slave owner was killed by a slave, the whole household of slaves could face death, even the innocent ones. Torture was routine where a slave was a potential witness in a court case. Yet even in Nero's time there's a public outcry when that law is invoked and innocent women and children are amongst those killed after a famous murder. Increasingly, the laws slowly shift away from treating slaves as things rather than people, albeit people in the bottom rank of society. By the time of Theodosius there are laws to keep slave families together. But if you're expecting the arrival of Christianity to end slavery, think again.

It's a social phenomenon, fighting against hundreds of years of tradition, involving huge numbers of people. It's much the same with gladiators. It takes a hermit called Telemachus at the start of the fifth century AD to physically drop into the arena and get in the way of the show to get things going. He then gets bludgeoned to death by the crowd throwing things at him, but then they realise what they've done and go home, and an Imperial decree ending the games follows.

So the good news is that slavery and gladiatorial games will still be in place during your visit.

We can't help thinking though that slavery may be holding the Romans back. They have all manner of inventions borrowed from the Greeks, like using running water to move wheels that turn and pump and grind. They are a wonder to find on those rare occasions that you spot them, like the waterwheel hammers of Britannia's western mines, but if you have slaves on treadmills who needs to design more wonders like these? Still, it's the Romans loss.

Gods Above

Religion

Crossing the gods can get you into all kinds of difficulties both with the powers above and with the civil authorities.

In the Empire, the gods are worshipped a bit differently from back home. There are sacrifices, particularly of cheap livestock, or foodstuffs. But there's next to no human sacrifice, which is considered excessive. That said, there have been famous instances in Roman history in times of crisis of human sacrifices occurring. There have been a couple of generals who dedicated themselves to the gods and plunged into battle in order to secure victory. There has also been a lunatic who rode a horse into a big hole in Rome in order to close the chasm. More troubling to the reader, on a couple of occasions Romans in the past sacrificed a couple of foreigners who happened to be in the wrong place at the wrong time when wars were going badly. It's very unlikely you'll suffer from it, thankfully. To be fair, in the past we have sacrificed more than our own fair share of Roman prisoners of war.

Although if you are mistaken for a Roman by Boudicca, you might find that old Celtic sacrificial habits die hard. Just like you.

We can divide religion up into several areas;

- Roman-Celtic gods
- Cults
- Beliefs, including what the free barbarians of the islands believe
- The group styled Christians

Roman-Celtic gods

When they conquer a country, the Romans like to assimilate where they can. This is not just the rulers; it includes aspects of their society, from styles of housing to the gods themselves. So as you wander the country you may find temples dedicated to entities that have both a Celtic and a Roman name., In cases such as these, the Romans discovered a local god and realised that it was, in terms of its powers and its legends, quite similar to one of their own gods: so they put the two names together and hey presto, Jupiter's your uncle.

Examples of this include Teutatis (Mercury or Mars), Sulis Minerva, Andate (Victory), Apollo Maponus, Belatucadrus (Mars), Cocidius Silvanus, and many more.

Often these gods are very local, so don't be surprised if you find a shrine only pops up in an old tribal area. Others however are more widely recognised and may even have come originally from far afield, and be familiar to a wider audience.

Then there are the spirits some Romans have borrowed from the Greeks and brought along with them. An example is the Agathodemon, a friendly guardian spirit, and the Kakodemon, which isn't.

The Romans are also keen, however, on abstract gods. These might be a quality, or they might be a state or a state of mind. Safety is a good one to be able to sacrifice to, for instance, and there's also Pax or Peace. Rivers, cities, and even continents can also be personified (they can often be seen on coins), and once recognisable in this form, it can be a short step to putting up an altar for the well-being of anyone travelling on old Father Tiber for example. There are spirits to which you can sacrifice if you have an issue with hinges, mountain ridges, stored crops, knots in plant stems, spreading manure (Stercoratio, if you're interested in a quick prayer), mildew (Robigus, which also demands a dog sacrificed when the star Sirius is high), or weed clearance. The Romans are quite mad about this. Sometimes you almost think if there was a shortage of carrots, someone would dedicate a shrine to some orange headed deity.

It is prudent, however, to keep such thoughts to yourself. While many in the upper classes may privately at times be sceptical of organised religion, the prevailing trend is one of belief. It is said that Julius Caesar was cynical, though certainly avoiding giving that impression in public. On the other hand, his successor Octavian(Augustus) was very superstitious. Once, the litter in which he was being carried was frazzled by a bolt of lightning, and a slave carrying a torch was killed. Afterwards, Octavian would carry a special seal-skin amulet for protection. Again, on account of a friend's dream he decided against staying in his tent during a battle, which proved just as well as the mattress was stabbed when the enemy broke through. He considered it bad luck first thing in the morning to put his right foot into his left shoe, but drizzle when starting a journey as a good omen. He refused to travel on market day, and avoided business on the Nones, since he disliked the sound of the name.

As a result, you may find it easier to avoid openly involving yourself in religion if possible. You can always when travelling stop in a wood and conduct an offering in private if the need arises at the start of a journey. Since as you are discovering the Romans have a god almost for everything, a compromise might be to stop by a location dedicated to the Unknown God if you find one. By definition, if the Romans don't know who this power is, maybe he is one of ours?

Roman religion can often be more formal than our own. Special buildings, or temples, are erected in which worship can take place. Alternatively, shrines can be erected in open spaces, such as in the forum of market place, or beside the road, or at a place appropriate for the fulfilment of a vow, such as overlooking a shipwreck site if a sailor makes it to shore. In Britain, you might find that some of these are in fact built on older holy spots from pre-Roman times. This is especially the case with respect to holy waters, often taken over to become springs and baths in the new age. Other candidates for special attention may be locations touched by a god, for instance by a lightning strike.

There is a special profession dedicated to looking after these locations, called the priest. He is responsible for managing the offerings, whether of animals or wheat cakes and wine, though the prayers themselves may well be provided by government officials. If you are attending, do so in silence. This allows the prayer reader to get the prayers right, and prevents ill omens from taking place by an unfortunate comment from the crowd. A flute player may assist in drowning out any background noise. Items sacrificed are left for the attendants to dispose of. On other occasions, feasts for the gods might be laid out on banqueting tables to which their images are brought.

In some cities, the priesthood may be a part time role, perhaps an honorary or even a political one as we have seen already with Julius Caesar who became Pontifex Maximus, a very senior priestly position. You are extremely unlikely to bump into any of the top ranking priests in Britain. At best you might spot a priest at a temple dedicated to a deceased emperor, and see a freedman from some imperial estates, but don't hold your breath in this country.

You certainly won't see one of the celebrated vestal virgins. There are only a handful of them, and they are in the city of Rome, doing their vestal virgining, whatever that entails. Don't be tempted to find out, as the penalty even for passing underneath her litter when she's being carried around is death.

Fortune Telling

You may be tempted to go the tourist route and visit a fortune teller during your stay. A number of people are credited with the power of predicting the future, and these are called soothsayers. This too is taken very seriously, with soothsayers consulted before many a great enterprise. In days of yore, one admiral called Claudius got into a lot of trouble when the sacred chickens refused to eat before an engagement; he declared that they should drink instead, threw them overboard, and went into battle regardless. He lost badly. The chickens did for his career. They did for the life of another man on another occasion, a sacred chicken keeper who lied about them supposedly eating. Confessing moments before the battle begun, he was immediately executed as an attempt to win the gods over.

The future can be predicted in a number of ways. A favourite is looking at entrails of animals when they've been sacrificed (the meat goes to the temple: don't try to walk off with it). Augurs are priests who use the Etruscan method instead, interpreting in particular the path of birds across the sky. More plebeian types might throw some things and review how they fall. A local old favourite is to let loose a hare, and see whether it runs on the favourable side.

Watch out for astrologers and sorcerers as on occasion you may find consulting them banned by imperial decree. That won't stop you spotting visitors to holy springs scratching curses on lead sheets and throwing them in, hoping that the gods of the underworld take note in their bubbly lair.

It's a different way of doing things than back home, where our own holy women determine the future by looking at how the eddies of the river flow; or have our holy people throw fruit twigs up and onto a white cloth to read

Mars is the god of war. Best to avoid pillaging his temples in case he takes offence.

how they fall; or watch the behaviour of our holy white horses. Romans don't hold much of our way of judging the future by fighting a prisoner as a token of how a future war will work out. A good German won't take these Roman tricks too seriously and consider it harmless fun, but you never know. Maybe it really will pay for you to beware the Ides of March...

Most popular 'standard' gods

Jupiter – King of the gods, god of thunder
Mars – god of war
Juno – goddess of childbirth, Queen of the gods
Minerva – goddess of wisdom
Neptune – god of the sea
Venus – goddess of love, wife of Vulcan
Vulcan – god of fire and smithing
Ceres – goddess of crops
Vesta – goddess of the hearth
Apollo – god of poetry, archery, divination and many more
Diana – goddess of hunting
Mercury – messenger of the gods

Cults

You might say that cults take two forms: the family cult, and the big cults.

Roman families are big on their ancestors, and on their own family divinities. The Lares and Penates are openly revered in a traditional Roman home. These are the spirits of the ancestors and the household gods. You might find them reverenced as little images or in a tiny shrine, possibly very ornately made indeed, in the home. A small sacrifice of honey might be an appropriate offering if you are staying with a family and are invited to join in.

The Manes are the spirits of the dead. These are honoured at the tomb, perhaps even by pouring offerings of wine in through a special trough and gap.

You are a long way from Capua and the home of the famous matres matutae where even the invading Hannibal paid his respects, but you might possibly encounter something that looks like them. These are stocky images of mother figures, sometimes seen in groups of three. It's an image that's been around for a long time across the whole continent.

Now, the big cults however are something else. The thing about a cult, however, is that its occult (meaning hidden) and its full of cultists, who are keen on keeping their secrets. Far off in the Greek world they are their groups keeping their mysteries, ceremonies that take place in private amongst the initiated. The author has never been to one, but it's reasonable to assume that they are about educating people about the hidden side of a particular god's background, exploring the meaning of old stories by use of metaphors and what things stand for, and fulfilling certain obligations to encourage for instance spring to come or the Nile to flood.

As a barbarian in Britain, it's unlikely you'll bump into anyone who'll admit to knowing much more about these things than you. They are, after all, mysteries. But some cults do get to Britain.

Don't crash them. They will take part in a darkened space, possibly underground, quite possibly with one exit, likely with a priest who is half way through doing something unpleasant with a knife when he spots you intruding on his sacred event. If however you are invited to attend, you will be told what you need to bring and wear, and given a little background as to what is expected of you.

The Cult of Mithras is a soldier's cult, and so if you are a low season visitor who is helping out with the army, you might, just might, possibly be invited to join if you keep your old religions to yourself. There are a number of temples that spring up across the province, often by army bases.

Essentially, it involves going into a dark basement, where a man with a floppy hat kills a bull, and there's blood everywhere. If you pay close attention you might recognise some activity representing the god stepping out of stone and being born, though it might be that to get the full experience you will have to pass a series of tests and become promoted within the order over time. Still, even a limited access visit to the rites provides a spooky experience that gets very edgy once the bull gets it.

Mithras is a traveller, in the sense that he originated from the east. Rome has long been open to foreign religions, including taking on new gods. The Senate imported Magna Mater, or Cybele, from Phrygia to guarantee it victory over Hannibal. It took the form of a black rock that was shipped over.

Awkwardly, the boat grounded in the Tiber and a vestal virgin had to manhandle it free: good timing on her part, as her actions disproved a claim of unchastity that had just surfaced about her. The new goddess brought with her a new way of looking at religious rites.

It is quite a shocking one for outsiders, because of the way you enter the priesthood with a number of these eastern religions. Take the ceremonies associated with Attis, Cybele's other half. On 22nd March, a pine tree is chopped down and carried to the holy place by a special troupe of people as people shower it with white roses and coins. The trunk of the tree is dressed like a corpse, and wrapped in violets to symbolise the dead Attis, and a little model of a man is also attached to the tree. The next day, there is a lot of horn blowing. On the third and final day, the Day of Blood, the chief priest cuts himself a lot. Others join in wearing frightening quivering head dresses. In the course of the celebrations, amongst all of the music and incantations, some worshippers become completely frenzied and chop off their danglies.

While the goddess was revered, the process that drove people to becoming such priests, or Galli, was not. It was long forbidden for Romans to take that route, though that ban has now been lifted.

It is possible that you might find a spot worshipping Cybele. If you do, we offer a strong word of caution. If you value your manliness, don't get too worked up in the worshipping. And if people start offering you sharp-looking pieces of Samian pottery to play with while holding something that looks like a giant walnut cracker, start running.

Not all cults involve dark cellars or man issues with cutlery. Another later cult is worship of the Sun. This has been around for a very long time, but the craze for new religions from the east encourages its resurgence and spread. For about fifty years up to the time of Constantine, it was even an official cult, perhaps helped by a strong interest in the army. Its profile was increased by massive personal support by emperors such as Elagabalus, who himself took part in ceremonies involving the holy rock that fell from the sky, brought over to Rome from Syria. But his attempt to merge their version of the cult with the traditional Roman sol invicta, or unconquered sun, didn't end with a unified pantheon, and new emperors brought new trends.

Beliefs

Organised religion apart, there are a number of superstitions and quirky practices a traveller might also encounter during his stay away from religious sites. We don't have space to highlight them all now, but you might for example come across a reference during a drought to the lapis manialis. This is an old stone kept near a temple of Mars outside of Rome, which when moved to the city triggers a shower of rain. If you spot an old-fashioned type breaking an egg shell or snail shell after eating from it, he's following an ancient custom to avoid wizardry being done with it. When travelling on a ship, don't get caught clipping your nails or your hair as you'll raise a storm. On the other hand, if you are sick, cut your nails and have them fixed to a neighbour's door with wax. He'll get your illness (only use on people you don't like).

Don't clasp your hands or cross your legs in company, particularly if you are next to an ill or pregnant person. This is equally so if you are at an important business meeting or religious event. Your posture is impeding things.

If you get into a conversation about local history, never ask about what the 'real name' of a city is. For those that believe these things, the city's home deity has its own true name, and priests on campaign would encourage a city's defending god to defect to the legion. Rome's own god's true name was a secret a certain Valerius Soranus paid with his life for loosely divulging.

If you have a hunting dog with you and it has some red-haired puppies that you are fond of, beware to whom you sell them. They may be intended for sacrifice to ward off the effect of Sirius on the crops.

You might overhear worried discussions about sacred trees. We Germans take these things far more seriously, most notably with our use of such things to nail the skins of our victims to. But we also share a common interest with the Romans in trees, especially oaks, that have been blasted by lightning, and there are two sacred trees in Rome itself. One is the sacred fig tree of Romulus, and the other a cornel tree on the Palatine. If either is spotted wilting, it creates a great commotion as a sign of immense bad fortune and bad news to come.

Ringing in your ears? Someone is talking about you. Want to avoid baldness or headaches? Cut your hair on the seventeenth or twenty ninth of the month. Don't remove someone's table or serving tray while they are drinking as that's bad luck. Mention the dead, and quickly add that you should not disturb their memory. Witness someone sneezing and you should quickly wish them good health.

You'll find a lot more, particularly in rural areas where older beliefs have survived more, and where people are less well educated.

Some of the oldest may involve harvesting, and racing not to be the last person to finish their allotted area of reaping. The loser may get some form of straw doll if they are as a symbol perhaps of the spirit of the corn. These things sometimes can be seen in some of our own lands too, whose meaning is lost in time, but hint at a blood sacrifice in olden days to guarantee good harvests to come.

The Old Faith

The ways of pre-conquest life live on, especially amongst those people who live on these islands beyond Roman power. Sadly, you won't spot a good old fashioned German goddess's wagon doing the rounds in the countryside. But if you are in lands that remember their Celtic past, one ceremony you won't want to miss is Beltane.

On the first of May, you'll find huge fires being lit on hills and exposed spots, since the gods don't live in little houses (as they see temples). A slice of turf is cut. A pile of firewood is made for the need-fire. There is a special procedure for this. The night before, all the fires in the neighbourhood are put out. An oak plank is produced. As many as nine people collectively turn a shaft set against the wood to start a flame by friction; these people have to be free of crime, or it will impair the process. Kindling is brought forth as soon as the signs of fire appear. The flames are considered magical, with powers over sorcery, poison and disease.

Everyone contributes to a communal meal. You will see a special cake or cakes brought out; the Beltane cake. Eggs and toasted oatmeal are popular versions, and they tend to have bumps on top. A starting rite might begin with food being thrown over the shoulder as offerings to various gods:just follow what everyone else is doing. Singing and dancing follows around the fire. A big

Beltane cake is divided up, for instance by people picking while blindfolded.

One unlucky person will get a special piece called the Beltane carline, which may be covered in charcoal to distinguish it, or be particularly knobbly. Some people then make play of trying to throw this person into the fire while everybody else restrains them, while in other places there is a pretend attempt to lie him on the ground and cut him into pieces.

Do check before attending this community event that the old practise of ritual sacrifice is not maintained locally, and the mock version is used instead, as otherwise your holiday might become as truncated as you are. If you do end up being picked, you might be expected to jump three times through the flames, though this should be allowed to take place at a time when the process is not a suicidal venture.

Afterwards, any food that is left may be taken away, but available for finishing later.

There are local differences. In the far north east you might find the fires happening on the second of May and called bone-fires, and rowan twigs put by barns along with small fires to keep evil spirits at bay. In some of the western islands you might see a special cheese which is kept as a form of charm, and cattle herded around the main fire, before people take some of it to their own homes. In the west, rather than jumping over one fire, you might find several people required to run between two. In Hibernia, cattle might be herded between them as well.

Whatever the version, a bountiful harvest is meant to follow. In any case, you should enjoy a quirky social gathering. Nor is the ceremony so strange when you reflect on our own customs, since many of our peoples also set up large fires at the start of May which we too dance around, and which are used to ward off evil on what we ourselves know as Walpurgis Night.

The Christians

The more you come back and visit Britannia, the more you may notice the growth of one cult in particular. The religion practised by those known as Christians is very different from anything known in our dark woods. It concentrates on the life of a wise man and divine entity, much of whose teachings are set out in writing.

Special buildings are set aside for worship, like temples but involving some form of pretend sacrifice using wine and a type of bread. If you do attend a service, do not carry out an actual sacrifice. This is very bad form and may lead those present to assume that you are involved with one of a series of occasional purges, or persecutions, generating (i) a panic (ii) the appearance of a few individuals who seek martyrdom.

Britain may be off the beaten track, and on the other side of the known world as far as the founders of this faith were concerned, but it does have a few fascinating religious individuals you may encounter. Albanus is a Roman soldier in Verulamium who takes on the official clothing of a hiding priest and pretends to be him to let him get away. His head is chopped off as a reward. Aaron and Julius are two other martyrs you might hear talk of.

Persecutions of this sort do happen occasionally. It might be worth being tactful on the subject if visiting while Septimius Severus is on the island, and during Diocletian's rule (though Britain is spared the worst thanks to his local co-emperor Constantius Chlorus pulling his punches). Decius in the middle of the third century also attempts to purge the state of the religion. By the fourth century, thanks to Constantine the Great, the religion gets a much stronger official footing and survives the brief reign of his relative Julian the Apostate: within fifty years, it is the official religion of the state.

As the saying goes, avoid discussing religion and politics. In this case, the two go together. If in a dinner party you hear people arguing about whether or not the shrine to Victory should be left in or taken out of the Roman Senate house, keep well clear. It's a controversy that will run and run. In AD 392, the issue is settled and only Christianity is allowed, and the old faiths become pagan ('paganus' meaning countryside, where they withdraw). You'll have to keep your blood-curdling beliefs to yourself when visiting from now on.

It's in this vein you should keep an eye open for a special man, however. In the fifth century, just at the time when Britain is slipping from the grasp of the empire, a monk appears by the name of Pelagius. A large and corpulent figure, he is extremely well-educated in religious matters, and speaks both Latin and Greek well (which should tell you something about the quality of local schools). He leaves these isles to travel to Rome and to the east, to take part in the great debates about faith. The viewpoint that finally won was that humans were born in a condition of original sin, and needed Christ to save them: it was a view that great Church thinkers of the time such as St Augustine and St Jerome supported. Pelagius, however, loses out on being St Pelagius because he holds the other view which would in time be seen as a heresy.

That view was based on the idea that man had within him basic appetites, but he was also divinely given a moral ability to control them if he so chose. Jesus's death was an example rather than a breaking of any actual law of the universe, since it was a personal failure of Adam in the Garden of Eden rather than something that damned everyone else. This all meant people could enter heaven by goodness even if they never found God. Of course, people who thought the Church – and particularly as it were, the single approved Church - was the route into Heaven might take issue with that.

A discerning barbarian does not need to be so discerning as to become more than passingly acquainted with the hugely complex issues around these religious arguments. Such disputes keep appearing amongst the priests of this faith with baffling complexity on trivial details. But it is useful to know that in Christian company if the subject strays to religion, in the low season and for a good century afterwards, you will find a number of people who think Pelagius was right.

A mosaic of the new god Jesus Christ that you might see in a British villa. The funny thing on his head is not a hat but a sacred symbol called the chirho. Photo: Andrea Rueda.

Special Considerations

Embassies and consulates

There are no barbarian consulates. It is extremely unlikely that there will be any visiting embassy either.

If you are in difficulties with the authorities, you are on your own. The best you can hope for is to quietly get word back via another visitor or trader from home, who can encourage a relative to 'bring the boys'.

I wish they all could be Caledonian

The Romans occupy parts of the far north on three occasions, and this may affect your scheduling. These are around AD 79-87 (Agricola), AD 139-165 (Antonine Occupation), and AD 208-212 (Severan Occupation).

Note that no towns or villas are built in the occupied zone, so don't expect to trade with any flourishing new colonies.

Travellers with disabilities

Visitors with special requirements will not have them automatically catered for, and given the state of medicine in our home lands will be genuinely lucky to still be alive.

Monsters

Seafarers will already be aware of the beasts of the deep and the threats they pose to shipping. But once you land, in the British woodland, there are a number of rustic creatures that create their own hazards. Fauns and similar creatures, while entertaining to listen to as they play their music, are associated with the God Pan. His parties are extremely rowdy and excessive. Don't challenge him to a musical competition as if you lose you will be flayed alive.

You may also spot a number of attractive women who live in trees and streams. We advise you to leave this pond life alone as they have complicated love lives.

The Romans also have ghosts, and necromancers. These latter are feared rather than respected, and their activities are often treated as a capital crime.

As for the Celts, their tales talk of a wild hunt that takes place, a chase by fearsome spirits, not unlike what we hear about back across the sea. If you hear a mighty crashing taking place, stay well clear of it lest you be taken up in it, perhaps even as the prey.

In the far north there are also creatures that carry axes, which resemble men with birds' heads and have a tendency to peck at your own, along with half-fish half-pig things and dog-headed warriors.

There are no trolls in Britain.

Wildlife

Whether you are hunting or just out and about, note that despite the civilising influence of the Romans, there are still familiar dangers in the local

The wild white cattle of northern Britain are a tough bunch, but the meat is excellent.

woods. In the far north you can find a wild cat, though this shouldn't cause too much of a problem. Wild boars as any reader will know can be ferocious beasts and savage with their tusks, even if favoured sport for hunting. It's not for nothing that these creatures pop up in poetry such as Ovid's, either involving them stabbing someone badly in the nether regions or just squishing them, or as the subject of some vengeful god who has unhappily turned a relative into a boar which some unsuspecting person then hunts. Sadly, the greatest beast of all will not be found. The celebrated Calydonian Boar, an ox-sized beast of literary fame, is named after the town of Calydon in the east - not Caledonia - so your chances of having to wrestle a giant the likes of which crushed great heroes of yore is nil. But the locals are large enough for a real challenge, and make tasty sausage. Even the manure has its uses, especially if applied on anybody involved in a chariot accident or otherwise badly bruised.

Wolves are a great pest to livestock farmers, and the large proportion of the countryside that is covered in forest provides plenty of cover. Be very aware of this danger in times of hunger, especially if travelling at winter. When passing roadside graves, observe to see if any bodies have been dug up lately. We advise you stay on the roads, and consider investing in a hound if you are likely to be camping in the open. If it comes to it, travel with a stranger who is slower than you.

Bears are another threat, though as they are also favourites for the keener hunters you'll spot a very marked decline in them, indeed finding them very rare by the low season. You should be familiar with how to deal with them as they are the same brown types you find back home. That means keep away from cubs, scramble up really sturdy trees to get away from them, and don't try to go fist to paw and outbrawl one, because you'll lose. The experts also point out that their breath is poisonous.

105

If you are lost in the wilds and truly desperate for a snack, note that the local squirrels are all of the red variety and live in trees. Adjust your traps accordingly.

There are some snakes but no scorpions. Roman survival experts recommend repelling them with the use of garlic.

No elephants have been seen since Claudius briefly brought them here. Being caught tracking one will end in ridicule. The paranoid will recall in any event that they are quickly tamed by giving them barley juice.

At sea, be mindful of the goby fish. Roman sailors will tell you that this tiny creature is capable of holding ships fast more securely than any anchor. You'll have to send a diver overboard to scrape it off before you can move.

Domestic animals

Some animals are kept as pets. These include dogs, some of which are very ugly and a lot more compact than the hunting dogs, and aside from being quite well treated almost as family members are often considered useful for guarding buildings at night. Small birds such as sparrows may be kept by women – you might encounter a famous poem by Catullus who writes about one. Peculiarly, domestic cats are increasingly to be found, an innovation the Romans are said to have originally imported from cat-obsessed Egypt. The two last pets do not necessarily get on.

The bond between the locals and their pets can be extremely strong, and this might be useful in selecting a kidnap victim during a raid on a villa. One false move and Fido gets it.

Culture

Music

Local music will seem strange at first. In part this is because of a very noted difference with the types of musical instruments available. Back home, travellers will be more familiar with instruments that are blown to make terrifying noises, and or that involve hitting something.

Happily for us, music is not as important here in Britain as you will find it in areas with greater Greek influence. If a musician is called upon in the course of a dinner at which you are a guest, it is advised that you smile pleasantly and diplomatically note that your lands "have nothing quite like it". If a slave is employed rather than the host in displaying his skills, it might be wise to disappear for a comfort break and hope the moment passes.

A number of types of excruciating instruments of torture for barbarian ears are out there. Twin joined pipes such as the Tibia, and the Fistula or pan pipes, create a rural melody such as shepherds in the old Apennines might hear. Rather than bowstrings, musical strings can also be attached to these weapons to create instruments such as the lute, harp and lyre. As these leave the mouth free, there is a risk the player might decant some words to accompany the "music".

Wind instruments are even adopted by the Roman army. Early on, trumpets are popular to signal orders over long distances and over the din of battle. Thanks to the incorporation of Sarmatian horsemen into the cavalry, you may later on encounter riders whose appearance is accompanied by a ghostly bellowing. This can be very disconcerting at first. If attacked by such a seeming fiend, stand your ground! The phantom calls merely emanate from a device attached to the dragon standard, and a charging rider or strong gust of wind channels this into noise.

Celtic peoples also use a form of war horn, or carnyx. You

might possibly find them being brought out at parties and special events. They certainly make a din. We tend to have an image of a long bronze boar-headed tube rising skywards amongst a mass of charging warriors, which are certainly around. But don't be surprised if when you surprise a group of locals if one of them whips out something ram's horn sized to alert his fellow villagers. The smaller version may be originally of a Hibernian design and have a hole in its side through which the blowing takes place, with some nobbly bumps and wavy line decorations at the large end.

People attending religious services should not be alarmed if a form of musical rattle is waved in their face at any point. This is the sistra, of Egyptian origin (and it should have stayed there), and comprising of a frame with cross-wires allowing interminable jangling.

Tambourines can be used to provide rhythmic accompaniments. Of more satisfactory substance to barbarian tastes, you may in a more outdoorsy environment hear trumpets and drums. It is considered uncouth to begin any dance or shouting at this point, particularly if a procession of dignatories is being announced.

It is possible that in certain huge public buildings such as an amphitheatre you may encounter the sound of a massive caterwauling bellowing. Do not panic, and keep to your seat, lest you become a laughing stock, because this may be a water-powered musical instrument known as an Organ. Equally, if you hear a plaintiff cry coming from a straight-legged creature being chewed by a man, attack neither, for this is an instrument known as the bagpipe.

Roman instruments are often more fragile than our robust versions, and for this reason, incidentally, do not make good improvised weapons.

Nightlife
Try the docks.

Shopping

Londinium is the place to be. It's not that it's historically the key city, since it's only the second capital, and that honour after a couple of hundred years gets split and then split again. It's not just that it's the biggest city in the land – it only just edges out the other provincial capitals on the island at their height. It's those reasons plus the fact it's down south, on a major river, and almost pointing straight at the rest of the empire.

Of course, the main trade routes run up and down the country. Pottery, glass, metalware and wine goes north, even north of the border; slaves, cattle, furs, animals go south. Metals, including lead and silver, join wool and grain in being sent back over to the continent. In Britain indeed, lead is counted so plentiful on the surface that there is a law limiting production.

If you're trading, plump for bringing over rarer furs for import or re-export, and there is always an eye open for amber. Here it's called glaesum, and is brought over from the German island of Austeravia for expensive women's jewellery. You may find wines here of slightly rougher quality than the established vintages further south, and thanks to the later growing season possibly a little more pert and less fruity, but it is as stupifying as the next amphora and will serve to get your German clientele just as drunk. You'll see a lot of these being loaded and unloaded at the port area, and here's probably as good as any a place to get some business done.

Roman jewellery is exquisite, and the empire provides an important conduit for rare and precious stones to transit from far off lands. Jewels are highly prized: Nero over in Rome watches his gladiators' fights reflected in a large emerald. Some are cut and mounted in rings, to create marks of authenticity in molten wax attached to documents and letters.

For shopping for fineries, try the forum. This is near to the basilica, where government sits alongside the law courts. As a marker as to the hustle and bustle you'll find another new basilica and forum being built only twenty years later, a mighty construction that's the largest building north of the Alps. Now that's money talking.

The Theatre

If culture is your thing, instead of anything quite so energetic as a hunt or gladiatorial show, plump for a visit to the theatre instead. That is to say, a visit to the theatre. If there's a score of amphitheatres dotted neatly across the land, for a proper bona fide good old style Roman theatre, with a stage and all the trappings, you'll have to go to Verulamium. Happily, there's everything you need when you come, with shops catering for your requirements. It's not all high drama, and you might find some of the earlier shows being a bit basic and rustic with dancing bears, wrestling and goodness knows what other forms of rudiments. But pick the right day and you might be in for a treat. Perhaps a farce, or a drama (see our box below on Roman authors for more on which performances you might wish to choose). Mimes, pantomimes, and displays of dancing are also quite popular.

Roman theatre can be very visually impressive. Theatre sponsors have long had a habit of going over the top to

Chariot racing is fast, exciting and great fun. Be careful about laying bets, however, some of the so-called sportsmen are a bunch of crooks.

produce an opulent and realistic effect, with large scale casts and masses of props. You're unlikely to find anything as extravagant as Nero's stages here in Britain though, where he simulated a burning house with an actual blazing building set, and recreated the fall of Icarus with an actor tumbling to his death.

Thinking of picking up a scroll to read? Try these Roman authors

Caesar – politics, and military history (of himself)
Catullus – depressed poetry
Cicero – statesman, legal speeches, philosophy and letter writing
Livy – history
Lucan – bloody action historical poems
Lucretius – heavy philosophy
Pliny the Elder – natural history
Pliny the Younger - letters
Sallust – populist history
Suetonius - history
Tacitus - history

Not everyone can read by a long chalk – in fact some emperors couldn't. So what about a piece of theatre? Dip into a performance from one of the following

Horace – lyric poetry
Juvenal - satire
Ovid – depressed poetry, stories about gods
Petronius - satire
Propertius – nervy poetry
Seneca – personally flawed philosopher who wrote plays
Statius – epic poetry
Virgil – heroic epic, countryside poetry

Many of these poems can be enjoyed as recitations, or through quiet reading. If you are attending a performance of one of the great poems, note that what's also 'epic' is their length. Take a loo break (or 'assist the clothing cleaners with their work') before it starts, especially if at a dinner party and the host is reciting. He may not be Nero but he might spot you leaving half way through.

The Circus

If you want to experience the thrills of the chariot race there's only one place to be. Camulodunum is the site of northern Europe's bona fide circus.

The day begins with a procession of carriages with gods in them. The crowd will quieten down, then cheer as their favourite deity passes them by. Then the track is cleared and the races begin, with the first one being the most prominent.

The chariots will thunder round the track in the direction of a wagon wheel moving left. If the audience suspects a false start, you and everyone else can appeal to the officials to start again by waving your toga (in your case, bellow and shake your cloak). Seven laps later and the first across the line is the winner.

You won't see any of Nero's extravagances or the vast scale of Rome's displays, what with ten horse chariots, or four-camel teams trotting by. But the speed and skill of the drivers should more than compensate, especially if there's a horrific crash since the cars are flimsy.

Chariot racing is fiercely competitive – and that's just the fans! Supporters get fiercely defensive about 'their' team, identified by a colour. It's probably wisest to avoid being judgemental about which colour is best, unless it really is a massive fight you're looking at starting. You may find some soldiers quickly on hand to suppress it, but it might be a handy distraction if your lads from the boats are planning a spot of commotion on the other side of town.

Practical Considerations

Languages

Holiday words
buta – house
dunum – fort
katrik – fortification
liro – sea
ouse – water
pen – hill
pren – tree
tref – farmstead

Things you might want to describe
amaro – crying
birro –short
bodyo - yellow
druko – bad
gurmo – dark
kani – good
kayto – wood
kotto - old
kwezdi - piece

Things we can't imagine you might need to know, but just in case
brokko - badger
kasnina – garlic

Things you might want to buy
banwo – piglet
bratto - cloak
esok – salmon
karbanto – war chariot
koligno – puppy
rowk – tunic
smero - berry

Worst case scenarios
durno - fist
lomana - rope
swanto - treasure

Latin is an inflexive language, meaning the form or case of a word changes depending on what it is doing in a sentence.

If it is the subject of the sentence, it is called the nominative. servus adest: the slave is here.

If it is the object of the sentence, it is the accusative. barbarus servum videt: the barbarian sees the slave.

If something is happening 'to' or 'for' it, then we call it the dative. barbarus servo it: the barbarian goes to the slave.

If it is 'of' something, then we use the genitive. barbarus solidum servi rapit: the barbarian snatches the gold coin of the slave.

If something is done 'by', 'with' or 'from' something, then the ablative form is used. barbarus capitem servi ensi abscidit – the barbarian chops off the head of the slave with a sword.

Finally, if addressing something, that something takes the vocative; permirabilis ensis, dicet barbarus – what a fine blade you are, says the barbarian.

Of course, in real life things get a little more complicated, what with datives of possession and ablative absolutes and all manner of intricate special cases. But that's what makes it fun to learn and a bit of challenge. Plus don't forget that for many of the locals, Latin is their second language too.

If in doubt, speak slowly, loudly, and just take your time half way through a word noisily figuring out in a suffocated yodel how many vowels the dative plural takes.

You might find a few useful phrases handy to get you started, so we include a few in our section on emergency latin (q.v. – which is short for the Latin saying you should look it up).

Latin of course isn't the only language of these parts. In less urbanised areas you'll find quite a lot of Celtic, which is also the language you'll need to use if travelling to the parts of these islands outside of Roman control. There are different types of Celtic, but they should be mutually basically understandable if you grapple with one.

A trader once told us that the words at the top of this chapter are those he thinks he heard used;

Don't worry about spelling: these were passed on orally so just pronounce them as they look and point to whatever you're talking about. Besides, the trader who told us might have it all completely wrong and what do we know - we've barely got to grips with enough Latin to write as well as your average auxiliary stuck on Hadrian's Wall. But it's a useful skill to have, since you'll often find a Roman scout carrying a message written onto a scrap of suitable tree bark.

Writing in Celtic

If you're reading this, you are already familiar with writing on parchment. But the Celts write on stone too. They have a system called Ogham.

Ogham is made up of lines carved along the edge of a stone, or running down a central carved line, so that each letter is determined by how many lines lie on which side of the 'crease' of the stone. It can also be read on its side. If you like a fancy secret code to take back with you, learn some Ogham.

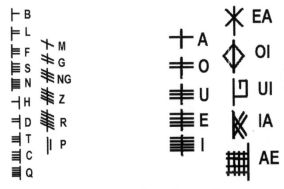

(P is additional – put that mark at the end)

You may find these letters, and the memorial stones carrying them, appearing more frequently in the Low Season with the appearance of numbers of Irish settlers in the west of Britain. You might even spot a number of inscriptions in both Latin and Ogham. Looking at one really does give you a feel of the social and ethnic complexities of the end of Empire, as the Celts of Britain reassert their identity, under threat from the invading Celts from Ireland, and as the Romanised Britons struggle to retain their own confused sense of place.

Working Abroad

Fighting with the Legionaries

Yes, the heading above is ambiguous, because we know that many of you will want to scrap with the Romans, but some of you will be after getting paid to fight alongside them. There's good money to be had in their service, with the prospect maybe even of a patch of land at the end of it.

In the high season, you'll come across a terrifying fighting machine. The early legionary is heavily armoured up top, with a short but lethal sword which is both powerful in the thrust and has a reputation for chopping limbs clean off. Don't expect to be able to lob back any of the javelins that they might throw at you, as they are made to bend on contact or have a wooden pin snap. In either case, you've got a lump of metal stuck heavily in your shield, and you'll probably end up throwing both away.

Watch out making obscene gestures from a distance. They have artillery that can throw rocks and cast bolts over unexpected distances with some accuracy.

They fight as a team and have high morale, unless you do spooky stuff to them (a group of druids or mad priests is a must-have accessory). They are well-disciplined, and protect themselves at night in a fortified camp built for the occasion, with a good gap between their pitched tents and the palisade to prevent you from trying to fire them. They'll level the camp again in the morning, so don't count on grabbing some cheap defensive real estate when they move on.

As time goes on, the legions also become more experimental with their equipment. They've always been good at engineering – Julius Caesar made a point of building a bridge over the Rhine just to impress the locals. The late army has all manner of strange equipment. A number of really whacky ones are starting to get talked about now.

There's the pontoon bridge, made out of hollowed logs

chained together and planked over. More adventurously, there's the bridge made out of air-filled bladders and covered with goats hair mats (ascogefyrus). Look for the horse-drawn artillery, or the armoured chariots (currodrepani) with adjustable scythe blades - very pseudo-Boudicca) that are variously designed for chopping up fleeing infantry. At the coast, keep your eyes peeled to see if anyone is going so far as to actually experiment with the special liburna, a huge ship driven by yoked oxen turning paddle wheels.

Your chances of joining this winning team early on are nil, because you are a barbarian. But they might be looking for auxiliaries, or assistant troops, to make up for the fact that they are light on cavalry and skirmishers, and to reduce Roman casualties in tight spots. Apply at any major military establishment. Being conscripted into the auxiliaries is indeed one of the complaints Calgacus makes when fighting Agricola, as they then get sent off to Germany.

The reputation of the legions in the low season is very different. Don't be fooled by the relatively low standards of the bored soldiers manning the frontiers. The field armies are much better, thanks to lots of aggressive campaigning, plus the occasional civil war. They don't have the armour they used to. Their shields are now oval rather than oblong. Cavalry is much more common. Even the use of the javelins is beginning to fall out of fashion, as soldiers carry large darts stored at the back of their shield. But despite these changes, it would be a mistake to consider the new legion with contempt.

This is just as well if your ambition is to join it. Barbarian nationalities can now get into the Roman army and serve in more orthodox units. You'll need to be around 5'8" for the cavalry or best infantry, though standards do slip and more emphasis is placed on physical strength rather than height. Some barbarians start doing really well for themselves, ending up as extremely senior figures and extraordinarily powerful men. Service in the empire is a way to prestige and riches, but it's also very dangerous at the top as power politics kicks in. Still, if you're serving in the British legions, chances are you'll not get caught up in any imperial politics – unless of course the legions suddenly go stir crazy and find themselves a local candidate for emperor. Then the sky's the limit for opportunities for plunder. We recommend you keep a good horse nearby and cut loose quickly as soon as your commander starts hitting a losing streak of battles though, as it all tends to end very messily.

This may explain why civilians start chopping off fingers to avoid military service, and why people caught trying DIY surgery then face being branded and conscripted all the same to make a point.

Military justice is brutal. Centurions don't just carry canes to point to things with. Punishment for breaches of discipline can be extreme. On the other hand, a complaint by a civilian sent to a military court (such as if you requisition their donkey and then sell it) may not get very far, so there's always someone worse off than you.

But then, maybe joining the legion is not what you are after. In which case, hit and run are the tactics you need. A quick unexpected descent in force on the eastern coast, ambush the reinforcements rushed to expel you, and run rampant for a short while collecting plunder before disappearing again. Try to time your arrival to coincide with activity by other barbarian raiders in other parts of the country, and you may end up temporarily causing a total breakdown of all law and order. By Wotan's eyebrow, the opportunities are magnificent.

Note that in early years the main weapon is a short sword, and this is worn on the soldier's right hand side, not his left, if you plan to grapple and pummel him. Watch out for a possible dagger on the other side though.

It may at some point be worth your while to note that the procedure for seeking to treat for peace is to stick your spear in the ground and to beckon with your right hand. This is a lot easier to arrange than hunting around for the classical approach of holding out a laurel branch in these parts. It is very bad form to apprehend let alone mistreat envoys during this process. You might find parleying a useful way of giving the enemy a chance to surrender or get out of your way.

One final but important point: many legionaries carry their money in a bronze purse they wear round their arm. Check here first on the body.

The Britons in Battle

If you do end in a brawl in the High Season, and are picking on an area beyond the current Roman border, note that the free Britons prefer infantry. It's possible in flatter terrain you might see some chariots, known to the Romans as esseda. These are a throwback to the old way of fighting and are a relic kept on in these islands. While the drivers are very nifty and can even run along the main spar, the ponies are quite small and scraggy and not up to pulling huge beasts of wagons with sharp whirring ironmongery nailed to the axles, so your chances of spotting scythed versions are sadly not good. Try the Persians for those.

Don't expect to see many in the rocky uplands, and in any event they are more of a prestige weapon since they are used by the upper classes. With rare exception, they are seen as forms of transport for a warrior to commute around the battlefield, allowing the occupants to get within javelin range before retreating again. The famous scythed wheels of Boudicca are a bloody exception but are flawed against a line of infantry with grounded shields. If you encounter one, stand your ground.

You'll probably hear a lot of shouting and some battle songs as the Britons advance. Actual charging will be dependent on where the bravest warriors turn out to be; anticipate a lot of missile throwing and skirmishing. A quick and impetuous charge before they psych themselves up for hand-to-hand fighting can pay dividends.

Britons are known, as with the old Celts, for their ability to swim across rivers alongside their horses and baggage. They seem to expect the Romans to always be building bridges, and repeatedly forget that the Romans' own Celtic auxiliaries can also swim across in the other direction too.

The Britons' weakness is their division. Old kingdoms in Roman times were divided up into factions and parties, and so formerly powerful tribes were incapable of fully uniting to fight off the Romans. Even getting two or three to unite was a major achievement.

Be wary, however, of taking on the Caledonians. Apart from anything else, they have less plunder, unless of course they have just hit a Roman site and you are looking at jumping them on the way back. In this case, steel yourself so that you don't lose any vital seconds in seeing a large naked man screaming at you. They still use chariots in the first century, and have small but fast horses. You'll see infantry who are capable of great speed but also good at holding a battle line. They have a shield and a small spear, at the end of which is a bronze apple that makes an unsettling clashing din when shaken. If disarmed, remember they often carry daggers.

Note that you will likely be encountering them on their home territory, and if seeking to withdraw to your ships they are capable of enduring hunger, cold and hardship to come after you. This includes entering swamps and staying there with only their heads above water for days at a time. In woods, they can live off bark and roots. They also have an emergency food supply which staves off hunger and thirst, although it only takes the form of something the size of a bean.

Meet and greet

Far from being a lonely isolated and distant outpost, Britain repeatedly hosts visits by some of the greatest men of the age, and yes occasionally some astonishing women. You don't have to travel to Rome to see the A list of the day, people like Claudia Rufina whom the poet Martial praises amongst the best of Roman womanhood for her beauty and brain. Despite being born amongst the 'woad-painted Britons', she even passes in the imperial capital for a Roman or Greek.

Time your visit well and you can coincide your stay with that of some of the most astonishing characters in history. The tragedies may repeat but it's never as they say reheated cabbage. Here's a selection of some of the most impressive.

A southern day trip: Gaius Julius Caesar

If you're going to start, coincide with a biggie! You can't get much bigger than Caesar, the man who conquered Gaul, bushwhacked the Germans, trifled with the Brits, and then went off and overthrew the entire Roman state and became its standing dictator (until he had a minor diplomatic dispute with some cutlery).

You will hear the name of Gaius Julius Caesar a lot. It is tactful not to point out he was a bald-headed weakling.

Caesar is a populist politician, who's already had some brushes with death at the hands of both his political opponents during a period of civil wars, and again at the hands of some pirates who, rather foolishly, thought he was joking when he told them he was going to execute them all. It's a measure of his stylishness that when first captured, he laughed at their massive demand for ransom and told them he was worth over twice as much. Fear means nothing to the man; he masks reversals of fortune as if always the master of the situation. A political gambler, he throws money around recklessly for political advantage, and so far has always been lucky at the way the dice have fallen. That probably explains his interest in military adventures, because war means lots of booty, and political immunity, and his debts are huge.

Caesar's a man of letters, and no mean education, having studied in Rhodes under the same teacher of public speaking as Cicero. This may help explain why some say his last words will be in Greek.

Mind what you say about his hair. He's very conscious of it, putting a lot of energy into arranging it when he has it, and hiding it underneath a garland of leaves when he starts to lose it (an award from the Senate he particularly values). You may catch his mannerism of scratching his head with one finger. Also avoid discussing family. Caesar's first wife has died, and he decided to divorce his second after a scandal when a man dressed as a woman was spotted at a religious festival held in his house.

Nor should you underestimate his physique. He looks pale and weak with headaches and even epilepsy, but he roughs it like any soldier and sleeps out in the open, travelling fast and snatching sleep as he goes. He's a good rider and even dictates correspondence as he goes.

His reputation has now already been established. They say he's stormed more than 800 towns, defeated 300 tribes, fought a total of three million men and killed a million (1.192 million to be exact), with another million taken prisoner. It's said that when the Belgae revolted in northern Gaul, the carnage was so great that the Romans could cross rivers and lakes on foot. It's only logical in this context that he's decided to come to Britain, as the first commander to launch a fleet on the Atlantic.

His expedition is a marvel to behold. In 55 BC, his forces suddenly appear off the British coast. Avoiding the cliffs, which had forces lined up nearby, he lands further down the coast. The men have a tough time of it, and it's not an easy scrap. The standard bearer has to set an example and take his chances rushing forward to encourage the others. A follow on battle is more of a close shave than the Romans normally face.

Barely is his army properly ashore than his fleet gets hit by a storm. The Britons attack, but while they are repulsed Caesar cannot pursue as he has little cavalry.

It's at best a bit of a no-score draw for the great man, so back he comes again the following year with not two but five legions. This time the ships –all 800 of them -have flatter bottoms so can be beached against bad weather. But again they get badly bashed by a storm. Still, the legions press inland and win some hard-fought victories against the locals' leader, Cassivellaunus.

A little incident tells you a lot about the sort of man in the army. When the leading centurions had stumbled into a swamp, a soldier dashes forward and does many heroic deeds in full view of his general, routing the Britons and rescuing the centurions. He is the last man across the water. As he makes safety, Casear and his generals shout out in amazement and approach the soldier, who falls to Caesar's knees weeping for forgiveness for losing his shield. This is the manner of men these Romans are. Although the fact these people execute soldiers who throw away their weapons may also have had something to do with it.

A flying visit to the island during this season will introduce you to the Roman army and its general at their best, really feeling the pressure. It's a moment of impressive spectacle and real adrenaline, on the eve of a massive Gallic revolt that reminds the world that the fighting spirit in conquered Gaul remains just as strong as with their cousins in Britain. Caesar himself has a reputation for bashing barbarians, including Germans, but off the battlefield he's quite open to understanding his enemy better. And how often do you get a chance to have a chat with a future god who's going to have a month named after them? Even if you miss the chance to meet him, there'll be no avoiding the fact that he's died. They say one of the omens of his passing will be the sound of battle in our distant German skies.

The Celtic Warlords

Caractacus

A hundred years later, and there's a worthy successor to Cassivellaunus. Cunobelin is a successor king, possibly his grandson, who cunningly avoids triggering Roman interest in his lands. After Cunobelin's death, a power struggle breaks out amongst his sons. It's enough to bring the Romans in as the anti-Roman faction gains the upper hand.

Caractacus, one of the sons, is at first just one of the leaders, but as the overwhelming power of Rome smashes opposition he becomes something far more. Fleeing the occupied south east, he heads west to lead the opposition there. In fact, he is not just part of the resistance; he is the resistance. For several years, he leads a heroic existence with wider renown.

When he is finally defeated and captured, he is taken off to Rome as part of a triumph. The custom is ritual strangulation as a sacrifice to the gods. But despite being paraded with his family before a mass of people who have come to Rome to witness the spectacle, rather than meekly submit he makes an impassioned speech: can you blame me for wanting to keep

124

my independence and riches, he asks, but well done for beating me. Claudius gets the point and spares him as an act of mercy. If you get to bump into him after this point, you'll probably find a very respected if very retired old soldier with whom you can share war stories, and maybe pick up a few tips.

Tiberius Claudius Cogidubnus

There were two options to Rome. You could fight it, or you could assimilate. Caractacus chooses the former, but Cogidubnus chooses the latter.

If you bump into him, do get back to us about his name. Some people say it's really Togidubnus. The merchant who told us did have a very bad cold so it's possible it's been badly passed on.

In the middle of the first century, Cogidubnus gets paid off with a client kingdom. This means he's allowed to run a large slice of the south coast, in return for being a loyal subject of the emperor (whose names, you might spot, he's taken on as a naturalised Roman).

Regardless of whether you catch him at the fantastically opulent villa at Fishbourne, if you are fortunate enough to be invited to a house party you can be guaranteed a thoroughly top-notch top of the range feast and entertainment on a par with anything the continent can offer. Maybe you'd better steer clear of politics, though: you might find a future emperor or two amongst visiting military staff on a nearby seat.

Boudicca

The fame of Boudicca, or Boadicea, knows no bounds and barely needs repeating here. She was married to a client king of the Iceni called Prasutagus, and when he died the family were viciously abused by the Romans. At this point, the eastern tribes noted the success we Germans had enjoyed a generation before in booting out the Roman invaders, and decided to have a go themselves. Steer clear of Roman friends in the south east from that point on, as a rampaging army will destroy its leading settlements, especially those that lack any fortifications (pretty much all of them) and offer opportunities for booty. Maybe 70,000 people die, often gruesomely including by crucifixion.

You're a barbarian: after a quick bit of DIY plundering, best leave the country altogether. The Romans will be back with a vengeance. Maybe 80,000 die. Boudicca is one of them, either by poison or perhaps illness.

Boudicca herself is an interesting character. You can spot her a mile off: very tall, frightening in appearance, piercing eyes, long reddish hair, a golden torc round her neck, a tunic of many colours and a thick cloak held by a brooch.

Don't get her annoyed.

Cartimandua

Less well known is this British Queen, who rules over the Brigantes in the north. Having signed a peace treaty with the Romans, she is allowed to continue to rule as a client queen. Not only does she keep out of Boudicca's revolt in around AD 61, but she also hands over Caractacus when he turns up after his defeat. That's what we call collusion. Don't trust her if it's a question of trouble with the neighbouring Romans.

If you're visiting, keep an eye open for some domestic issues. The word is that Cartimandua is looking at divorcing her husband, King Venutius, and marrying one of his arms bearers. You can imagine the sorts of problems that will cause if it happens.

High Season

Tiberius Claudius Caesar Augustus Germanicus

When Claudius visits Britain, he comes as the first reigning Roman Emperor to ever visit these islands, and he does so to put his own stamp on the conquest of the south of the country and to claim the prestige that comes along with it.

But what a fascinating character he is. He had a very popular father, Drusus, who died when he was young: the first general to sail the northern sea and beyond the Rhine, so perhaps the north is in his blood. Yet Claudius's own reputation before his accession is very low as people keep saying he lacks common sense or intelligence. On the other hand, given the politics of his predecessor and nephew -the increasingly mad Caligula, having a stammer and a reputation as a book worm probably saved his life amongst all the Palace intrigues. Still, hopes of a sound reign start from a low base. He is put on the throne by the Praetorian Guard who find him hiding behind a curtain.

So you can see why a successful campaign in Britain will add to his prestige, especially if he's in charge of it.

Claudius looks very imposing, at least when he's stationary. He is tall but not slender, has an attractive face, and white hair. But he has weak knees, an odd way of laughing, and when he gets angry he froths at the mouth and his nose runs. His head is very shaky and he stammers a lot. His eyes are often bloodshot.

Claudius is very proud of his family, so do raise the subject of his father when in conversation. It's from Drusus that the emperor has inherited the title of Germanicus. The army still holds a ceremonial run around his monument every year and a number of cities of Gaul offer prayers and sacrifices. Don't be casual with your oil lamp, as he has already had one house burn down (the Senate bought him a new one). Don't discuss mules: his guardian for a while was a muleteer who beat him, when he was young and considered backward. If he nods off, don't put slippers on his hands so when he wakes up he scratches his face with them: people used to make fun of him in that way years ago, but these days he can order executions.

There have been attempts on his life, and security is

extraordinarily tight around this nervous man, so leave your weapons behind if you are invited to dine. Even a dream could get you killed as a safety precaution. Still, he has been known to like a drink and a spot of gambling and board gaming (he's even writing a book on the subject) so the evening may be quite light-hearted. Avoid playing games at the table involving throwing food. It is said his eldest son, Drusus, died when he choked on a pear he threw in the air and caught in his mouth. You might spot children of guests sitting on the arms of the couches, as of the old way of dining. A dinner might be cut short if he gets hit by heartburn, which he gets very bad bouts of indeed. It is said that he has considered allowing flatulence during these events, owing to one guest risking his life if he restrained himself. Avoid the mushrooms: he's very fond of them, but we just have a bad feeling about them.

If you are there to do business, and he swears something "by Augustus", you can be assured he really means it. You can probably catch him in a good mood at a gladiatorial display, which he's a huge fan of, especially the really bloodthirsty ones. But beware also as he is subject to serious mood swings, ranging from the intensely diligent to the rash and heartless, and some people do abuse this. You'd best remember in particular the incident at Rome when the German ambassadors went and sat down in the same row of seats as the Parthian and Armenian ambassadors, next to the senators. Claudius let them, but you're probably not an ambassador so don't try your chances. Especially as he's been known to improvise gladiatorial matches during lunch breaks for carpenters if the arena props failed to work.

Under no circumstances ask how his wife is doing. His first fiancee he had to split up with on political grounds; his second became ill and died on his wedding day. His four marriages end up messily, with two divorces and an execution. His fourth was to his niece. It's a dangerous conversation to be had with an emperor. Stick with the fact that he's just invented three new letters of the Latin alphabet, even if they will get forgotten.

If it's action you want to witness, the campaign in Britain has plenty of it.

There's tension: the troops at first refuse to go, until Claudius's own freedman Narcissus steps forward to incentivise them on behalf of the emperor. A joke from the ranks on the irony of a lowly ex-slave giving them orders, like during the Saturnalia festival, breaks the ice and motivates the men.

There's action: the tribes fight many battles, on two occasions defeated only because the Roman's own Celtic auxiliaries from Gaul swim across a river and start attacking horses rather than men, leaving the leaders as exposed to defeat as their warriors.

There's spectacle: Claudius himself now arrives bringing with him more impressive forces including elephants (these are giant walking whales, never seen before or since in these latitudes). Camelodunum is captured and the south submits.

The triumph in Rome will be spectacular, with provincial governors and even exiles recalled to witness the emperor ride through the city in a chariot, followed by others who had won awards, and the rest in purple-bordered togas. He'll also celebrate by sailing into the Adriatic on a special floating palace.

If you don't get a chance to meet him, you may still come face to face. There's a good chance you'll find a statue to him in a city centre. As another Roman leader who gets deified, and who has a personal attachment to the province, his image does crop up here and there. In the new Roman capital of Camelodunum in which he ends his campaign of conquest, they even build a temple to him when he's gone. The symbolism is so strong that it's a prime target for Boudicca's men, who burn it – and the fugitives inside it – to the ground.

Titus Flavius Vespasianus

One of the generals serving in Britain at this time is Vespasian. His background is worthy but hardly noble, coming from a respected background of junior military officers and taxmen, including one who retired as a banker in the country of the Alps. Strongly built, he also has the look of someone straining: once when he asked a wit to make a joke about him at his expense, he was told that he would once Vespasian had finished relieving himself. He's a fan of ball games and has a bit of a common 'street' way of pronouncing certain things.

By the time of the British wars, he has already achieved some political success. The campaign will make him. He fights thirty battles, reduces two strong tribes, seizes more than twenty towns and takes the island of Vectis off the south coast. As a marker of this success, he will get two priesthoods, the triumphal regalia, and a couple of months as consul. It won't be a climb fully to the summit: his future lot is to take a low profile to avoid political intriguing by Nero's mother, and his first posting after that leaves him nearly bankrupt and having turnips thrown at him during a riot. But his

reputation is such that he is the one sent in to suppress the Jews during their revolt, which will put him in charge of a large military force just when the civil wars start after Nero's death.

Vespasian is an emperor to respect. One of the toughest soldiers ever to wear the imperial diadem.

It will launch him to the imperial throne. But at the time of your visit to Britain, he is here as a commander of a legion – a senior military figure, but one of a number.

Vespasian is a modest man, aware of his relatively humble origins. He is not paranoid, so you won't automatically get the full body search treatment. You can expect a fairly frank and free discussion, but he's certainly not a fan of the cynical philosophers. He does love his money, so be cautious about saying you pay either too many trade taxes or not enough. Then again, he is generous with his friends so you may personally profit from his acquaintance if genuinely maintained, or at least enjoy some sumptuous dining with excellent musical entertainment.

Check under the furniture when you are dining. One of the omens of good fortune he had was when a pet dog brought back a hand from a cross roads and dropped it under the table. Not so much good luck for the original owner, though.

Don't discuss street cleaning with him. When Vespasian was aedile in charge of street cleaning in Rome, Caligula thought he wasn't doing his job properly and ordered his men to cover him with mud. He's also the emperor that in time will tax public conveniences. His son Titus will challenge him: Vespasian holds a piece of gold from the first tax take under Titus's nose and points out the money doesn't smell. Don't be too offended if he nods off either. He'll yet doze off during a performance by Nero and that nearly will be the end of him!

Titus Flavius Vespasianus (junior)
Titus is Vespasian's son (confusingly, they share the same full name so some outsiders refer to different parts of their names). He was brought up alongside Claudius's son, Britannicus, and indeed it's said he sipped a little bit of the same poison that killed off his friend.

He's short, extremely strong, and has a big belly. He's a good rider and swordsman and a capable poet and musical performer. With luck, you may get to see a display.

He's serving alongside his father Vespasian in Britain, just as he did in Germany before now. There's one report that he saves his father's life. The reputation he makes is such that they are already putting up busts and inscriptions to him. He'll spoil it with a bit of a reputation for fast living (and you'll need to be quick to keep up) and also cruelty, though in fact these may turn out to be a bit exaggerated.

Titus will go far, to the imperial throne in fact, if only for a couple of years: a happier destiny than his uncle Sabinus who also comes to Britain, but who will be executed in Rome during the civil wars.

Publius Ostorius Scapula

Claudius's generals may have laid the groundwork for a Roman Britain but two men really set the foundations in concrete. The first is Ostorius. He's the second governor of the province, taking over from Aulus Plautius who returned to Rome to celebrate an ovation for the initial conquests.

It's probably best to avoid discussing his predecessor. That's not because of any personal issues; after all, Ostorius if anything gets a slightly better level of public acknowledgement for his work. But back in Rome Plautius's wife, Pomponia Graecina, will run into trouble for following some sort of strange cult. Some even say it's this extremely new fangled Christian thing. Aulus takes advantage of ancient Roman law to try the matter in-house and acquits her. But it's all very racy stuff and they might even one day make for fascinating literary characters, since you have to ask yourself with the real life story line, quo vadis? It also makes you wonder if there is any tiny chance she snuck over with her husband, and bumped into someone on pastures or mountains green.

But Ostorius has a tougher job ahead of him than Aulus did, dealing with a strong British fight back. Thanks to some

A statue of Ostorius wearing full Roman armour. The man rarely had time to wear anything else given the constant fighting in which he was involved.
Photo: Ad Meskens.

excellent generalship he smites the wavering Iceni and crushes troublesome Brigantes, securing both as client kingdoms. Then he's also responsible for a spectacular defeat of Caractacus in very difficult terrain. Despite these astonishing victories against tough odds he then blows things. His troops, thinking things are won, get slack, and get caught out in several local defeats. Then he suggests that the tribe of the Silures that Caractacus had been leading should be wiped out or broken up and transplanted. Not surprisingly, they don't take too kindly to that prospect and fight all the more vigorously. The war drags on and Ostorius dies, it's said, of fatigue – a sad end for a former consul.

Give him some allowances therefore if he cuts short any dinner with you to get to bed early. Happily, you might find another interesting character also in your company, Publius's son, Marcus Ostorius Scapula. Ostorius junior is awarded a civic crown no less, a military decoration for saving the life of a fellow citizen, during a battle with the Iceni. He too later makes consul, under Nero. He's a big man, and a noted soldier. But he'll end his days having fallen out with the Emperor and living in exile in Northern Italy, where Nero's men come for him and tell him his time is up. It's rather ironic as it's because he's been caught checking his horoscope with a famous astrologer to see how his stars fare. Not well enough for his ambition it seems.

The big man, it seems, has a reputation that makes him a threat in an age of political plotting. He's not alone. At least he gets to outlive the son of his father's predecessor as Governor of Britain, Aulus Plautius. Some say it's because Nero's mother fancies Aulus and thinks he might make a decent emperor. Whatever the truth, in either case, being a second generation quasi-Brit does nothing for your health as we'll keep finding out.

Gnaeus Julius Agricola

Agricola is the name of just one of Britain's many governors and military commanders, but perhaps the most celebrated. In part he has his son-in-law, Tacitus, to thank as his biography is an enduring hit. But there would be no story without the amazing Agricola himself.

He served his military apprenticeship here in Britain years ago, as a tribune greatly respected by Gaius Suetonius Paullus. This Suetonius was the remarkable general who would crush Boudicca, later end up as Consul, and be a prime backer of Otho during the civil wars. His immense military reputation went unheeded: he recommended delay when fighting fellow claimant Vitellius. Otho disagreed, fought, and lost.

Standards had dropped in Britain after the Boudiccan revolt, partly to reduce tensions but also in part because discipline in these distant legions wasn't what it used to be. With Vespasian on the throne and the civil wars over, order was restored and local forces pushed into the troublesome northern tribal lands. Agricola himself now reappears, and astounds the locals with a surprise attack on the troublesome island of Mona by sending some auxiliaries swimming across the shallows.

Like Vespasian, Agricola is a modest man, downplaying his successes. His appearance is described as graceful rather than commanding, but his style gets results . He sorts out the grain market and ends exploitation of farmers, traders and buyers. He supports the establishment of temples and courts. He educates the sons of the nobility, introducing a love of the toga, the Latin language, the bath house, and dining. As Suetonius says, what they call civilisation in fact is just another part of their servitude.

Agricola's campaigns take him to the distant north, beyond the rivers Clota and Bodotria that almost cut the far north into two. The Caledonians are terrified by the presence of a fleet off their very shores. They gather an army of said to number 30,000 men under Galpagus. The deciding battle takes place at Mons Graupius. Although outnumbered, the Romans push back their opponents, and a dangerous attempt to swamp their flanks is beaten off by the cavalry reserves. The slaughter that follows is terrible, though an ambush by rallying locals in the woods is narrowly avoided.

If in social company with Agricola, don't discuss his family. In the latter stages of the war in the far north, he is busying himself to distract from the fact that his son has just died. His virtuous mother was killed in the civil war by Otho's marauding fleet. You could discuss the large role his German auxiliaries played in the front line at Graupius, however, which could get you some brownie points.

You won't have much chance to discuss his victories, as with the army returning to winter quarters, the governor is now recalled. The news of this success has travelled back to Rome, where Agricola is honoured. But the emperor Domitian is a worried man. In Agricola he sees a possible rival. It doesn't help that other wars across the empire are going badly wrong. Agricola retires to a private life, where he will pass away.

Publius Aelius Traianus Hadrianus Augustus

The Emperor Hadrian is a monarch who travels across his domains. A visit to Britain won't keep him here for long – a few months. But it leaves a psychological mark across the north of the country in an enduring physical form.

Hadrian is Trajan's heir and successor, having married his niece, a succession that marks the continuation of the golden era of the Roman empire. This was a bit of a fix given that Trajan hadn't exactly agreed to the arrangement before dying, but the palace settlement worked. It did take a couple of years for the rule to settle down in Britain, however, which probably goes some way to explaining why he turns up here in AD 122, and why he orders the troops to busy themselves by building a brand new fortification eighty miles long.

Despite the talk of some nastiness that happened when he came to power, when you meet him you'll find him a pleasant and charming man, a fond student of Greek and Latin, and a keen model maker, amateur architect, and painter (he seeks to excel in everything he does). Don't though demonstrate you are better than him in anything as this might make him angry if actually true. He is astonishingly jealous, and he has killed someone for pointing out an obvious design mistake of his. He even tried to abolish Homer.

Even so, he is quite capable of recognising individuality, such as the herald in the gladiatorial games who quietened the crowd not by shouting as ordered but by simply raising his hand. There's also the case where a woman made a request as he was passing by travelling. He told her that he hadn't time, and she told him to stop being emperor then. He stopped and heard the case.

Don't discuss family matters. He'll be sacking some senior court officials soon for being less than proper towards his wife

Sabina than formalities demand. If he hadn't succeeded to the throne thanks to his marriage, he would likely be dumping her too. Be very cautious in any letters you may write to any of his staff, as he spies on his friends and associates. You might also need to be discreet as he has affairs with some of their wives as well.

In Britain, you'll find him surrounded by the top men, travelling (relatively) incognito in a litter (you might be offered a lift if he knows you are are going to the same place). He keeps to himself on public holidays, breakfasts without wine, and drops by on sick friends. He hunts (pranging a shoulder and hurting his leg in the past), once killed a large boar with a single strike, and for his favourite hunting horse Borysthenes even set up a tomb with an inscription when it died.

He'll visit all the various military sites and investigate not only the ramparts but also the garrison conditions of the soldiers themselves. If you're an auxiliary, be prepared to endure a quick chat about your lot, but hide away anything luxurious before he drops by the accommodation block. You can also expect a lot more training when he is in the province. If he finds out you're German, expect some questions on local politics, as he'll soon be looking at appointing a king there.

Hadrian has his faults, but a visit to Britain during his visit provides an outsider with a good review of the empire at its height of organisation and relative peace, in the company of a man considered flawed yet still one of its more capable and measured rulers. Traders should enjoy it while it lasts, because the season for rampaging is on its way.

Mid Season

Ulpius Marcellus
This is a remarkable general for many strange reasons. He has been sent here by Commodus to deal with a major invasion

by the Caledonians after they had beaten up an army and killed its commander.

He keeps his appetite in check by a very peculiar policy. He only eats bread baked in Rome, which is quite stale by the time it gets here. This makes his weak gums bleed so he can't eat much of it. He also has a habit of sleeping very little, but increases his reputation for alertness by prepping messages for his officers that would be sent out in the early hours as if he were still awake.

He's highly competent, incorruptible, but equally haughty and quite horrible. He is also extremely ruthless. His talent will narrowly later spare him the executioner under Commodus.

Unless you have to do business with the man, avoid him. You won't like his table much.

Publius Helvius Pertinax

Pertinax is a very stern man, which you have to be in command of a legion, but also personally very gentle and considerate. It's a combination that almost served the empire extremely well.

Pertinax's claim to fame comes at the end of his life. After the death of Commodus, he ascends the throne. He will last under three months, in which he will grapple with an empty treasury, corruption, and a breakdown in military order. He will be murdered for his efforts, marking definitively the break down of the Roman empire's gold standards and the opening of generations of fairly constant civil strife.

His earlier links to Britain might have given him some advance warning of the problems he was going to face. In around AD 185, legionaries in Britain elect one of their officers, Priscus, as their new ruler. Priscus tellingly informs them that he is no more an emperor than they are soldiers! They then proceed to send a fairly large armed delegation to Rome to complain to the emperor in person. Surprisingly, rather than wipe them out, Commodus listens to them and decides to agree to their demand to execute one of his leading men, Perennis, who was effectively running the state.

Given these developments, Pertinax is recalled from forced retirement and instructed to restore order in the British legions. It's a region in which he had served as a junior officer some years before. He spends a couple of years doing just that, and in the process almost gets lynched. It was a tricky posting as the men seemed to want to declare anyone Emperor, with Pertinax himself top of the list. He suppresses a mutiny but, it's said, is left for dead when almost killed in another.

He punishes the rebels very severely, gaining a bad reputation for tough discipline that leads him to request a transfer. He gets it and leaves the province. But while he improves on his skills of maintaining order with an unruly army, he never quite grasps just how far gone is discipline and that all it takes is for one soldier to buck the curve and draw his sword and strike. You can request a transfer from Britain, but you can't transfer away from being emperor. Pertinax's time in Britain is an advanced echo of the huge disaster and tragedy that will shortly hit Rome itself.

Decimus Clodius Albinus

Clodius Albinus is the first man who seeks the imperial crown from a British power base. He takes over from Pertinax as the governor. If you are serving in the ranks and have an opinion on Pertinax as emperor, either remembering his discipline or happy that someone who knows Britain is now in charge, keep it to yourself; Pertinax's days are numbered. He gets killed off and an astonishing auction takes place at the camp of the Praetorian Guard between two candidates trying to outbid each other to buy the empire. The winner is Didius Julianus, but at either end of the empire other candidates are also acclaimed – Clodius Albinus in Britain, Pescennius Niger in the east, and Septimius Severus on the Danube frontier. Severus captures Rome, and wins over the German legions, badly weakening   Clodius Albinus's position. Clodius Albinus decides to ally with Severus, in return for being named his successor.

Severus secures the throne and Clodius Albinus is left on in Britain. But big tensions remain. Severus seeks to set up his son as his heir, while Clodius Albinus has been sending dodgy letters looking around for allies.

In AD 195 Severus makes the split, but it is Clodius Albinus who makes the running. Don't volunteer for this campaign. He pushes into southern Gaul in AD 196, where there is a massive battle. Severus wins and Clodius Albinus is pushed back, and captured more dead than alive. His head is stuck on a spear and his trampled and decomposing body left to the dogs and then dumped in a stream.

What sort of person will you meet if you visit during this period? He is a very military man, with a solid background in fighting barbarians (including, it has to be said, Germans), and an interest in letters including composing poetry. He's strict, plain-acting, and generous (though with a measure of self-interest). His opponents put it about that he is gluttonous, and a huge fan of figs, peaches and oysters available in massive quantities – some nice melons or grapes might be an appropriate house warming present. Some say that he's quite cruel, drunken, well-dressed and a philanderer, but that may just be gossip by his opponents, so take it with a pinch of salt. His tastes seem to change, for example he can go for a while without drinking at all.

He's tall, with wild hair and a big brow. He's extremely pale, with a bit of a high pitched voice, and a reputation for getting angry easily. By the time you'll encounter him in Britain, he's quite old. If seeking an audience with him on some business matter, don't carry any hidden weapons as there is a genuine threat of assassination from Severus's envoys as the political scene gets worse. Do though discuss his family pedigree, as he comes from a solid old Roman family.

Lucius Septimius Severus Augustus

Clodius Albinus's vanquisher is Septimius Severus. Having beaten the man who ran Britain, he comes to the island in AD 208 to sort out the administration and keep the troops busy. Not for nothing does he gain the title of Britannicus. He restores the Wall, and hits hard the northern tribes – even women and children are being slain.

Severus is originally from North Africa. He is austere, hard-working, and takes his job very seriously, once said to have beaten an old associate for embracing him familiarly while on public duties. He dresses plainly, with a shaggy cloak and very little imperial purple on his tunic. He likes African beans, some wine, and is a light meat eater. He has a long curly grey beard, a face that inspires respect, and a clear voice with a marked African accent. He is short, but strong, although becoming very weak through gout. He is not very talkative, but very attentive.

He has a reputation as a good administrator, but lately has at times been

It is best not to cause trouble when Septimus Severus is about. He tends to kill you first, then ask questions afterwards.

cruel. A lot of Albinus's people are being executed still, including his family, so it's best to make sure you're well and truly distanced from the old regime.

He has a personal interest and some skill in astrology, so perhaps you might ask him to try a spot of divination on your future (while remembering he has the power to cut it very short if you are annoying him).

You might be invited to a social gathering. His wife, Julia Augusta, at the end of his life was in conversation with the wife of the Caledonian Argentocoxus. The empress made fun of the Caledonian habit of the women being free and easy with numerous men. In return, the native suggested that the Celtic way was better since it was done openly with the best men, while the Roman way was doing it in private with the worst.

This being the acting imperial capital, you might also come across some of Roman society's leading figures of the day, such as the hugely important lawyer Ulpian, whose work will form the backbone of established law codes.

Don't discuss Severus's stay in Athens years ago. He had a run in with the locals many years ago and has had it in for the city ever since. Beware of making any jokes, as he is easily slighted and has no sense of humour when the joke's on him. Don't inquire as to the current stories about the infamous bandit Bulla, who is running rings about the Italian magistrates, shaving off half a captured centurion's hair and sending him off with a message that the emperor should feed his starving slaves before they turn into bandits. The whole thing is a huge embarrassment right now.

Don't ask him about his health either. He is coming down with a terrible disease that will kill him.

You might spot an incident if you are in the western area of the Wall. Coming back from an inspection, wondering what omens he might bump into, he came across a black soldier who was a celebrated jokester, carrying a garland of cypress boughs such as are associated with death. Severus took the omen badly, especially when the soldier then told him to be a god. Arriving in town, thanks to a misunderstanding with the local priest, he was taken to the Temple of Bellona (goddess of war, rather than peace – their priests slash their arms: very messy) and ominous black sacrificial victims were presented. Severus left in disgust and the livestock followed him back to his doors. One bad omen you can get away with: the gods were really pointing the finger on this one.

He'll die in Eboracum in AD 211, declaring that he has left the empire at peace, even in Britain, and carrying out administrative work even to his final moments. He gives this deathbed advice to his two sons: "Be harmonious, enrich the soldiers, and scorn all other men."

His body, in armour, is placed on a pyre and his sons and soldiers run around it in order, flinging objects onto the flames. His remains are carried back to Hadrian's mausoleum at Rome. That, sadly, is the trigger for some rather nasty in-fighting, and Britain lies at the heart of it.

The Family of Severus: Geta, Caracalla, and Elagabalus

Caesar Publius Septimius Geta Augustus, or Geta for short, is Severus's younger son. Caesar Marcus Aurelius Severus Antoninus Pius Augustus (and then some), or Caracalla, is his older. They do not get on, at all. In fact, that's a prime reason why Severus has brought them to Britain, to try to teach these brothers how to.

He fails. Britain becomes the hub of imperial plotting, and Eboracum the capital of the Empire and the heart of the imperial court.

Geta is attractive, to the point without being rude, and a bon viveur. But he is also merciful, thoughtful, affectionate, but with a stammer despite a clear voice. He wears bright clothing that his father makes fun of. Don't expect to get any nice presents from him, it's not his style. A quirk you may have fun spotting is during dinners, if he serves food beginning with the same letter of the alphabet.

Caracalla is reserved, stern, harsh-looking, and arrogant. He likes talking about Alexander the Great, the emperor Tiberius, and the dictator Sulla, pointing to how cruel he could be. He is gluttonous and drinks a lot, though on campaign does the same work and eats the same food as the troops. His name comes from the long hooded cloak he makes fashionable, so say something nice about it. Avoid comments on chariot racing, which he takes so seriously he will later execute a retired famous charioteer called Euprepes for having won 782 races, but for the wrong team. He can be generous, sometimes unexpectedly so if there is humour attached. But he is also obstinate, and greedy of power. Not for nothing does he come to enjoy the nickname of the 'beast'. Even if you've met him in Britain, avoid him when he comes to Germany; he kills a large number of volunteers after putting out that he's recruiting auxiliaries.

Caracalla as emperor will be most famous for his edict that soon, in AD 212, will make every free born person in the empire a Roman citizen, including everyone here in Britain. He will need the popularity. Don't suggest that too openly: he has spies everywhere.

After Severus's death, Geta and Caracalla share the empire. But both are ambitious, and their personalities clash. The court splits. The brothers leave for Rome, but the presence of the legions who want to see them work together prevents murder. It doesn't last, and Caracalla stabs Geta in the presence of his mother during a meeting that is supposed to settle their differences.

A killing spree begins across the empire, with 20,000 associates and supporters of Geta butchered. If you got on well with Geta during his visit, now is a good time to get out of the country. Heads will roll in Britannia. This really is so not a good time to be around.

144

Varius Avitus Bassianus, also known as Elagabalus, is the fourth family member who will wear the imperial purple, whom you might just spot in Britain at this time. His grandmother is the sister of Severus's wife. We shall avoid commenting on his strange religious and lifestyle choices, which will shock many in Rome. Steer well clear of his parties if you happen to make the capital: even Caligula would think them wildly excessive, with lots of flaying and death and dismemberment and things. At this stage as you visit Britain he is only a child in the imperial court. Children: sometimes don't you wish they just never grew up?

Give the provincial changes a couple of years to settle in, and you may find Marcus Antonius Gordianus Sempronianus running the northern province. He'll be emperor for all of three weeks as Gordian I in a couple of decades' time. I wouldn't count on investing too much in his dynasty either – he outlives his son, meets his end by the end of a noose made out of a belt, and his youthful grandson (after showing considerable promise) dies lamented after six years. But Gordian's presence does slightly add further to the impression of retrospective imperial lustre.

Marcus Aurelius Carinus Caesar

The son of the emperor Carus, brother of future joint emperor Numerian, Carinus campaigns in Britain and is awarded the title Britannicus for his efforts. It is said he has his vices (don't let him stroke your beard), though has a rather fine entourage of dodgy women and pantomine artists to keep everyone entertained. He loves jewels, and even has jewelled shoes. You will enjoy his banquets as they have masses of food, fruit a go-go, and even roses from Milan. His plunge baths are kept cold by using snow.

Carus will die in his tent of an illness during a thunder storm, leaving his two sons on the throne. Once again, don't volunteer to join any British expeditionary force to support the imperial candidate. Numerian is murdered soon after, and Carinus ends up overwhelmed by Diocletian.

Do, however, turn up to any public shows Carinus might put on; the family are renowned for some marvellous spectacles, such as people running up walls to escape from bears, and a large mechanical stage. You can recognise the man himself by his bald head and curly beard.

Gaius Flavius Valerius Constantius Chlorus

When Diocletian splits up the empire into four, in the system known as the Tetrarchy, Constantius I Chlorus is appointed to sort out Gaul (which has Germans sitting in it), and Britain (which has a pretender sitting in it). He achieves both. In AD 296, he invades Britain. Fog in the Channel both muddles his plans and those of his enemy. His opponent is defeated and he seizes the island. He returns ten years later to beat up the invading Picts alongside his son Constantine, but dies in Eboracum in AD 306.

Chlorus is like many emperors of this time of very lowly background, and to secure his position he has had to marry the daughter of his boss rather than the mother of his son. It's best to avoid this touchy subject, since some see Constantine as illegitimate.

Chlorus is very pale, has a face like a pointed shield, and is a religious moderate – he mostly ignores the persecutions of the Christians the Emperor Diocletian has ordered him to carry out. If you point out you're not a Frank who's come over pestering Gaul, you may get on well with him.

Made in Britain

Marcus Aurelius Mausaeus Carausius

Keeping the North Sea free of barbarian pirates in the late third century is a man by the name of Carausius. Carausius is a famous Belgican. He also becomes famous for not handing over all of the loot he grabs from the pirates he nabs. Before the emperor's men grab him, in AD 286 he scoots to safety and decides to go it alone. He grabs Britain and the important North Sea fleet for himself.

Carausius is a bull of a man with a huge neck and a bit of a Neronian look to him. His luck holds out, with one invasion attempt failing, until Constantius Chlorus is appointed to get him out. Chlorus besieges him in Carausius's continental foothold in northern Gaul. However, one of Carausius's commanders kills him and takes over the usurper's throne for himself, in AD 293.

As a barbarian, in his presence make sure you distance yourself from whatever tribes have been doing the latest raiding (probably Saxons). If cornered, you might chance it and point out he wouldn't be half the man he was today if your fellow pirates hadn't been half a fine as body of looters that they are.

Something Something Allectus

The man who kills Carausius is Allectus, his head of finance. This makes it the first time the tax man takes direct control of the country. He has a more jutty chin and Grecian beard look than his predecessor. He doesn't have much more luck though. Despite keeping watch for an invasion, fog gets in the way and his fleet waiting by the island of Vectis is powerless to intercept. Some of Constantius's men under Asclepiodotus manage to land. A battle takes place and Allectus is killed. Constantius too now lands and finishes the business, obliterating some retreating Frankish mercenaries who had been pillaging Londinium. The revolt, and the period of an independent Britain with its own emperor, is over.

Be cautious of the money in this period. There are a lot of fakes doing the rounds, and some of the official material was made up of whatever bullion was lying around, which is of mixed quality. That aside, this is a good time to be doing

147

business if you can bring in luxuries from the Roman towns in Germany, since the normal trade might be a bit hit. On the other hand, don't get too close to the top brass, and make sure that come the end of the ten years of independence, you've got your valuables in moveables rather than property that angry Romans from the mainland won't come and trash when you're doing a runner.

If you find out Allectus's full name, let us know as nobody we've spoken to has any idea.

Caius Flavius Valerius Aurelius Constantinus Caesar

One of the greatest figures in world history starts his path to world glory in these islands. Constantine, later 'the Great', is the son of the co-emperor or 'tetrach' Constantius I Chlorus whom we met above. He's with his father in Britain to campaign against the Picts. But his father dies, in Eboracum (which is starting to get a reputation for dying emperors by now).

Before passing away, Constantius declares him a Caesar, or junior co-emperor. But this isn't how the system is supposed to work. Constantine sets out from the Palace in purple. He leads a funeral procession with his father's friends. There's a magnificent ceremony that highlights the achievements of the dead emperor by a man already displaying his own.

The soldiers – impressed, looking for a bonus, and remembering the father - swing it: they proclaim their support for him. It's 25 July, AD 306.

The trigger is a German king in the audience called Crocus, who leads the call. He's the commander of a cohort of tough Alemanni. You're not called Crocus by any chance, are you, reader?

Constantine won't stay long in Britain after that other than a couple of flying visits – he has wars to fight against Germans, and then against his fellow emperors. But if you're there in Eboracum on that day, you'll witness a key decision that sets in train a path that ultimately leads him to the throne as sole emperor over the whole Roman world, setting up a dynasty that dominates the next half century, founding a new capital at Constantinople that will last a thousand years, and establishing the Christian church with an agreed credo as the dominant and later the sole religion in Roman lands. It is the trigger for a massive revolution and the end of all that was before.

Constantine is magnanimous, bold, but increasingly attached to a formal ceremonial way of doing things you'll have to grin and bear if you want an audience. He is personally generous, interested in literature, and a supporter of public morality (so leave your wenches at home).

Don't mock his hairstyle, even though it looks like it's been cut by a blind man using a pudding bowl. Don't mock the Christians or wear huge religious symbols, given his father's own restraint towards them which might have been passed down. Don't complain about the sunshine as some think he has an interest in the sun god. Don't ask him about his father's wife, as that's not his mother. Do point out that though German you're not a Frank, whom he's already looking at beating up. Hopefully you won't get to see his cruel side, which emerges a bit later on as he gets single-minded and autocratic. Do also point out that Christians have fled periods of persecution by living amongst barbarians, so maybe he knows this person Marcus whom you met once. If he likes you, he might just honour you with a title and gifts and you might end up staying.

Flavius Julius Constans Augustus

Constantine's son, Constans I, visits Britain in AD 342, daring the trip in winter. Now's as good a time as any to spot a real emperor at work.

Or possibly not. Despite some early promise, like his

149

colleagues he does have a reputation amongst his critics for putting pleasure before business.

After Constantine the Great's death, several brothers became joint emperors. One of them purged the family of possible threats. Two years ago Constans duffed up his brother, Constantine II. His mother, Fausta, died suspiciously after the death of a half-brother, with possibly some adultery involved too. So don't mention the family. He is good at hiding his feelings, therefore don't take him at face value either.

On the other hand, he gets on well with barbarians. You might end up with a job offer, which you can exploit to harass the natives to your heart's content on 'official business'. But don't stay on too long if you accept. Having all these barbarians around annoys the locals. Back over in Gaul in AD 350 the senior officers get invited by some plotters to a birthday party, when one of them called Magnentius wanders in dressed in imperial purple. Constans does a runner till he's killed making for the Pyrenees.

Flavius Magnus Magnentius

The man who does over Constans I is an army commander by the name of Magnentius. Wait for it: he's half German (his mother is a Frank), and half British. How's that for your chances of getting a promotion! It's a bit ironic really given Constans's problem was that he had too many barbarians knocking around. But at least he knows Latin.

Magnentius is pretty even handed, tolerating pagans after a fifty year stretch of rough handling by the God Squad. This might account for some of his popularity. But it doesn't quite swing Divine Providence in his favour. There is a massive battle at Mursa just east of Italy, in which tens of thousands of Romans kill each other. It's an horrendous scene, with fighting going on into the pitch dark. Even if you're on the winning side, which isn't Magnentius by the way, your chances of walking away are fifty-fifty. You'd have to be a blood-crazed maniac to volunteer for the fight if you knew what was coming, but then maybe you are. He withdraws to southern Gaul, and dies by his own hand.

He's a sneaky character. He manages to win one battle by letting it be known to the opposing officers that he intends to fight them in an open space, but then ambushes them in a pass while they are casually marching there. He is one for show: you can always spot his tent as it is wonderfully marvellous. He's bold when successful. He's praised for being an open and good man, though his enemies claim it's just a show. Mind out with his mother. Though she's a fellow German, she also has powers of divination and can predict the future. We're not sure if he gets his cheekbones from her, but the image we've seen of him makes him look like a toad hit by an ugly stick. Maybe it was a bad artist. Or maybe you need to know not to stare.

Sadly, Magnentius's defeat means the winning Emperor Constantius II becomes supremely powerful, and slips into dark ways. There are informers everywhere again. It's not a safe time for you to be around.

Flavius Theodosius

The future Theodosius the Great (and future Orthodox Saint) accompanies his father, Theodosius the Elder, to Britain to restore order in AD 368. It's a brilliant time for rampage before he arrives. There are barbarians piling into the country from all angles; the local Roman forces have been badly biffed; top commanders have been killed – it's prime time grab and bag season.

The elder Theodosius changes all that. If you hear he's in town, leave immediately. He's stabilising the country and sorting out the chaos. It won't do him much good: a few years down the line he'll be executed probably because of politics. His son will go into retirement, until the disaster of the Battle of Adrianople in AD 378 when the Goths overwhelm the Eastern Empire and he's picked to rescue the state, which he does remarkably well given the circumstances.

If you can impress him during his stay in Britain, drop him a note now as he's employing barbarians (since there are so many dead Romans). Don't get him angry: he can commit atrocities if he's miffed.

Theodosius will also be the last Roman Emperor to rule over a united empire that includes Britain. It's the end of an era when he goes. But that's jumping ahead because of an usurper.

Flavius Magnus Maximus Augustus

Now we are approaching the end of the show as we come into the time of Magnus Maximus. Maximus is Spanish, and you spot him soldiering alongside Theodosius during the British crisis. He takes it personally when Theodosius is appointed emperor in the east since he considers himself just as good, and gets the soldiers to support his own bid. During a scrap in Germany his opponent's forces gradually desert and support him, so he wins there and kills the 'official' local emperor Gratian. Though he's recognised in that job, he then tries to grab Italy too. Theodosius's forces surprise and capture him.

After Theodosius takes back control across the west, he's only in charge for a few months. Then he dies and splits the eastern and western empires for the last time. In Britain, it's downhill from here as several usurpers take control.

Out of Season

The soldiers in Britain now get back to their bad old ways. The barbarians are running rampant on the continent and there's fear of them coming over unless a strong leader is picked. Marcus is chosen, but the troops then find he is not to their taste and kill him. He is followed by Gratian. Four months later, the soldiers do it again - now it's the turn of Constantine III, a lowly soldier.

Constantine has greater ambition. He leaves Britain and invades Gaul. He loses two generals in battle, and appoints to replace them a Briton called Gerontius, and a Frank who lives in Britain named Edobinchus (see already how the opportunities are opening up!). These are famous for their military skill, and smash their way through Gaul. Between them they push back the German invaders, stabilise the Rhine frontier, and seize Spain too.

But just as he was recognised as co-emperor by Honorius, who's busy trying to chuck Alaric and his Goths out of Italy, along come the Germans again and run riot across Gaul. Since much of the army is in Spain, the Britons and their neighbours are forced to defend themselves heroically. This isn't what they signed up for, and since no-one else is protecting them they decide to drop Constantine. Magistrates are expelled and they choose their own leaders. Constantine's power base begins to crumble and fall apart.

That still leaves Britain independent in AD 410. The emperor in Rome never is able to establish, or seize, direct control again. There are too many barbarians running over Gaul for starters.

There's trade, and you can still find goods being brought along the established trading routes – from Byzantium even. But the story is becoming one of a mixed land. With it come new legends, such as the betrothed German princess from Britain, spurned by her fiance Radigis, who raises a fleet and an army of Angli and invades Germany to go get her man – Britain's answer to the Trojan story. But that's a history for a later guide book. The shadow has fallen on Roman Britain. The end of empires is here.

Where to Visit

Visitors will have their own reasons for coming to Britain. What now follows is a short guide to help you with just a few of the highlights, and some of the easier targets. We can't hope to cover every town and city, but these will give you a flavour.

Note that we have followed the now-standardised practice of the unconventional explorer Wilfrid the Plastered in referring to the island as sitting essentially on a north-south axis, with the Picts in the north.

The Gateway Towns

Arriving from the continent, the chances are you'll enter by the towns of the south east. As these lie in the part of the island pointed straight at Gaul, you'll also find these urban centres form the basis of an ideal short stay. The region is fertile, the climate is pleasant, and travellers can explore a taster of the grandeur of the Roman empire in the space of a short amount of time if that's all they have.

Dubris (or, as it is known elsewhere, Dover) is one of the key ports. It lies nestled in amongst the daunting white cliffs that confronted Caesar when he first saw this part of the coast. It's an important trading harbour. Peering down over the town you can see the first of the brace of lighthouses, eight stories high and shaped like a knobbly blunt spear. This means that travelling in poor weather or caught by night, the first glimpse of the island you may get will be the flames from the tower guiding you in. You might find on arrival that you're wearied, especially if the crossing's been rough. Happily, the town's mansio provides a surprisingly opulent and relaxing place to unwind before you set upon your land travels. Its wall paintings are on a par with the best in the island and some of the finer works in Italy itself. They have a Bacchus relief, providing you with a hint of the vaunted wine the place has to offer. The place is central heated and has all mod cons. Avoid disappointment and come before AD 270 however, when the military knock it down to expand their fort. This is, after all, an increasingly important naval facility and defence takes priority. There is a military bath house, but we recommend you avoid it and its sailors.

Rutupiae is the other port you may come in by. If Dubris is the tradesman's entrance, Rutupiae is the official front door. It dates back to the start of the invasion itself, though its military phase didn't last long and now you can see an amphitheatre and of course the necessary mansio. Make sure you try out some of the celebrated local oysters while you're in the neighbourhood. What really makes the place stand out, however, is the gigantic triumphal arch you'll have to step under. It's ninety feet high, gleaming white, and topped off with statues. After a couple of centuries however this place will be turned into a military post, and the arch and mansio will go, to be replaced with a bath house, so this is definitely a high season visit unless you are a fan of earthworks.

Some say the land of the ancient Cantiaci, Cantium, is the most verdant territory in all of the island. It is certainly true that if you can only manage a short stay within both Britannia and the empire, you can do far worse than here, a corner of the island that combines beauty with civilisation. Indeed, while you are visiting why not make the most of your stay and see if you can for a short spell rent an actual Roman villa. When in Rome

If so, then we strongly recommend Crofton. Once a small rural farmstead, there are at its height twenty rooms, a terrace, and of course a hypocaust system that can be fired up if the weather turns. Two chambers have opus signinum (concrete) floors, and another three have tesselated floors, so you get a feel of culture under foot. The site is on a busy farm, so as you go around you can watch the workforce going around their business on the large estate of 300 iugera (500 acres). Plus it's not that far from Londinium - 11 miles or so - if you need to spend a few days there, or want to copy the rich locals and use it as an out-of-town retreat. It's open from about AD 140 to 400. Book before the collapse of civilisation.

> **Notes for out-of-season travellers**
> Crofton villa is handily sited right next to Orpington railway station. Details on the site can be found on the dedicated website at http://cka.moon-demon.co.uk/villa.htm. Opening times are restricted, and we recommend that you check to avoid disappointment, but essentially run from April to October – Wednesdays and Fridays 10-1 and 2-4.30; Bank Holiday Mondays the same; and first Sundays in the month (only) 2-4.30 but including a guided tour by an archaeologist. Additionally, there's a local museum nearby with material on a bath house:
> http://www.bromley.gov.uk/info/200070/museums_and_galleries/357/bromley_museum

Durovernum Cantiacorum (Canterbury)

Here it is: if you have only a fleeting moment to taste Rome, step away from the garrisons and business of the ports and visit the nearest best settlement with all the heady flavours of Empire.

When the Romans came to this part of Britannia, they changed a way of life for good. Locals moved down from their hill fort and settled in a proper town, swiftly becoming an important early hub. Give it time and the traditional huts give way to new forms. There's a baths house but far more striking when it comes in the late First Century is the theatre. When this gets rebuilt a century later its four stories will vie with anything grand anywhere upon these shores, and its broken hulk will likely overshadow the streets long after the Romans have gone. While you are in the town centre, admire the Corinthian columns supporting the neighbouring temple. It speaks volumes that its builders and backers chose such an elegant style rather than simply throwing up whatever would keep the rain off. It speaks something of a pride in the town.

The great city of Durovernum Cantiacorum is worth a visit to see the towering theatre, but don't try to attack it. The walls are well manned.

Notes for out-of-season travellers

Canterbury's Roman Museum is open Monday to Saturday 10-5, and Sundays (June to September) 1.30-5. See http://www.canterbury.co.uk/Canterbury-Museums.aspx for more details. You can find it on Butchery Lane. A key attraction is the inclusion of a large slice of a Roman house – the museum itself is peculiarly underground. Of particular note are its mosaics, rare cavalry harness fittings, and collection of Roman silver spoons from a Christian hoard, though the reconstruction galleries (including a villa room) make it considerably easier to picture what such sites originally looked like.

City Defences

As you're exploring Durovernum, now's an excellent time to look at how the Romans defend their towns. You may not be trading your wares the next time you're on a visit; you might find the gate doors not flung open quite so welcomingly.

There are several key things to note. First, expect a sentry, and probably a sober one. Security is taken seriously and the guards are professionals, subject to strict discipline (including the death penalty for snoozing on duty). Second, the walls are sturdy and high. You're not going to vault them, so come seriously prepared with ladder or ropes. Bear in mind with some towns there may be ditches that need crossing first as well. Watch out for those dug at a distance; they may be there to slow you for artillery to pick you off at a distance. Third, the weak point is obviously the doors, but anticipate sturdy carpentry. A couple of the team running up to them trying to barge them down will only leave you with a couple of winded team members. A lot of towns in Britannia will end up walled, so the simple lesson is for quick raiders to go for easy targets like the smaller settlements or lone villas.

The Roman baths can be confusing places, but copy what the locals do and you should be alright.

Or you can chance your luck with a walk round the circuit. In some places putting up walls seems to be the responsibility of the person who owns the land, so if you can pick a patch where they've scrimped a bit (or even not bothered), you might have an easier time getting in.

If you get a chance to sneak a spy in to look around a town in advance, make sure he observes what the local guard unit is. Whether you're facing a cohort of veteran legionaries with their throwing weapons, a detachment of auxiliary archers, or a band of fellow German mercenaries, is obviously going to temper how you approach rushing, sneaking or bribing your way into the place.

Notes for out-of-season travellers

The picture shows the entrance to Canterbury known as Ridingate. Sadly, much of what remained of the structure, modified over the years, was taken down in the late eighteenth century and a large part of what stands there today is a replacement from that era. Even that though is mostly hidden by repair work done after the structure suffered collapse in the early 1960s...

The Canterbury Archaeological Trust was formed in 1975 to undertake excavations, research, publication and the presentation of the results of its work to the public. The Trust's primary charitable aim is to 'promote the advancement of public education in the subject of Archaeology'. One way in which it achieves this is through its Archaeology in Education Service with a range of learning opportunities. Importantly, it also undertakes outreach, presenting at public events such as exhibitions and conferences, and is an active partner in various community archaeology projects. Members of staff give talks about their work and teach on a variety of university courses.

The Trust's address is: Canterbury Archaeological Trust Ltd, 92A Broad Street, Canterbury,
Kent CT1 2LU, Telephone: 01227 462062. Those interested in its work in the community can discover more via its website,
http://www.canterburytrust.co.uk or explore its Facebook page,
http://www.facebook.com/CanterburyArchaeologicalTrust

Londinium

Londinium's early fate was to share the disaster of Boudicca's revolt, with everyone who couldn't flee with the governor or the general's visiting cavalry meeting a grisly end. But the disaster merely accelerated the rise of this well-sited city, lying where the upper reaches of a navigable tidal river approach its lowest ford.

Unlike many other parts of the country, the place has a very civilian feel from an early age. This is a place of administration rather than a garrison, and its easy access makes it an obvious site for merchants coming in from the continent.

Geographically, the city is divided in two, with an east end and a west end marked by a stream some call the Walbrook.

As you travel around the place, you'll quickly spot that the living heart of the city lies around its main streets. The roads aren't as impressive as the ancient thoroughfares you'd expect in Italy made up of hefty blocks, but are more like large gravel paths. You might be a bit surprised by some lack of military precision with the planning of the smaller streets, which look a bit haphazard. Keep an eye open at night for the drainage ditches, which you can cross at one of the planks. If you're invited round to an ordinary worker's house, don't expect anything too grand just because they're a Roman. The entrance section might be timber, and the mosaics if they have them rather bland. A poky little place next to a shop might be what's in store, though as an honoured guest you might get some fresh meat if they have their own little kitchen garden and backyard.

The Forum, marginally to the east of the geographic centre, is where you'll find the business being done. Coupled with the basilica, the whole complex makes up an astonishing building, probably the biggest you're likely to see unless you travel as far as Italy. In addition to the imports and raw goods coming down from the north, you'll be able to do your key shopping here for your basic necessities. Local pottery, glass and leather are on sale, so now's the time to try on those new shoes you were after. For bigger investments, look for the larger fancy shops or go direct to the port area for the two main riverside storehouses to buy in bulk for export. Note than turnaround is fast so get your orders in quick.

Those seeking divine inspiration will not be disappointed. The city hosts a variety of temples, including a handy underground temple to Mithras. For the religiously curious, it's also one of the main Christian sites and in Constantine's time you might bump into the bishop, Restitutus, who has good links with the new emperor.

Away from the city centre, and you'll find the larger dwellings. There's an amphitheatre, to the north west of the centre, and after it's been rebuilt in stone from its wooden origins might be the ideal time to dip into this bloodthirsty entertainment – though take some waterproofs just in case (even the arena has had a drain put in it to keep the rain from lingering and stopping the place from hosting naval battles). The gladiators' battleground sits by the fort the military use to keep watch on proceedings. Other parts of the outer urban area also see concentrations of industrial workplaces: you'll be able to smell many of these before you see them, especially the tanners. Check before booking your accommodation that your lodgings are at a suitable distance if you want a good night's sleep and an undistracted stay.

Not all of the city sits together. The settlement extends south of the river, though getting a waggoneer to drive there after hours can be problematic. This spread helps to explain why Londinium has become Britain's biggest city, filling over 300 acres, and surrounded by a lengthy wall that's twenty feet high. But its political importance drops as the province is divided up into smaller administrative units. From the third century onwards it's past its glory days, with a smaller population and less-moneyed people to throw up such marvellous buildings. Indeed, in the fourth century a number of the public buildings are getting knocked down, even in the age that it receives its final honour of getting the additional name of Augusta. But nevertheless, as an enduring provincial capital and site of key financial administration, including for part of the time a mint, it stays on the must-see list for all travellers for as long as there's a Roman Britain.

Shadwell

Not all of Londinium is thrust and bustle. There are parts of the settlement where life away from the law courts, markets and deadlines allow for a more measured approach to life and a calmer sojourn.

If that's what you're after, consider staying a little out of town, a short distance beyond the walls just north of Wapping Island on the far side of the cemetery. It's more homely and genuine being away from all that marble and stone anyway and sleeping beside timber and brick. Plus you have all the convenience of only being a mile and a half walk from the heart of things and sited close to the main east-west road. On top of that, its river access means it makes for an excellent halt if you are a late arrival straight off the boat.

The settlement is particularly useful in having one of Londinium's four bath houses that we know about, which is sited next to the large square tower that dominates the immediate skyline. Plus you'll find a number of other traders in the same boat as you (almost literally), so you can exchange tips and talk of where there are calls for goods and services across town and further afield. All in all, it makes this community a microcosm of the trading opportunities across the capital, and across the entire province.

Those who fancy taking the plunge, but who are only in the province for a brief trading visit, should definitely make use of the baths. They are surprisingly spacious, and while hardly palatial some effort has clearly gone into making them agreeably functional and certainly good enough to be the

preferred haunt of some wealthy female patrons.
  Mind the black rat, though. We call him Nero.

Notes for out-of-season travellers

The Shadwell site has been the subject of detailed archaeology rather than being a site easily explorable. But the work done to date has started to revolutionise our view of London.

Those wishing to know more about the excavations can uncover them by reading A Roman settlement and bath house at Shadwell: Excavations at Tobacco Dock and Babe Ruth restaurant, The Highway, London, by Alistair Douglas, James Gerrard and Berni Sudds. It provides a fuller context for the illustrations and what the site means. This is available from Oxbow books or directly via Pre-Construct Archaeology through its website: www.pre-construct.com. Alternatively, contact the Publications Manager at Unit 54, Brockley Cross Business Park, 96 Endwell Road, Brockley SE4 2PD

Heading West

Travellers heading out of the capital and to the west at some point will need to cross the river Tamesis. The likelihood is that you will do it at Pontibus, known also to us as Staines. As the name suggests, the location is an excellent place to marvel at the Roman ability to construct roads across running water. The place has long been settled, but in many ways the building of the road and its bridges will prove vital. You'll spot the place declining a hundred years after the bridges are built (hold your nose as you pass the gravel pits; they are now a dump), but come what may the road and the bridges build travellers, and they keep the economy going. If you stay for any length of time, do ensure in renting a place that you are above the river's flood range.

Heritage. Copies of Up Pontes, which contains more on Roman Notes for out-of-season travellers

Tourists seeking to explore more of Roman Surrey can dip into the dedicated website, www.exploringsurreyspast.org.uk, run by Surrey Heritage. Copies of Up Pontes, which contains more on Roman Staines, can be obtained at Spelthorne museum which has a case dedicated to the town in its Elmsleigh Room. David Bird's book Roman Surrey and the Spoilheap Monographs on Roman and Mediaeval Staines can also supply more recent findings.

Visitors seeking to view finds from the area can obtain opening times and other details from the museum website, www.spelthornemuseum.org.uk. The museum is at 1 Elmsleigh Road, Staines, Middlesex TW18 4PM: Telephone: 01784 461804, and for would-be retro traders has a replica Roman shop, in addition to changing monthly features.

Opening Times: Elmsleigh Room (the History of Spelthorne): Monday, Wednesday, Friday 9am to 6pm, Tuesday & Thursday 9am to 7pm, Saturday 9am to 5pm; Thames Room (further displays and Museum Shop): Wednesday & Friday 2pm to 4pm, Saturday 1.30pm to 4.30pm

Away from Roman style towns, you will find old style Celtic houses still dominate. If the locals don't give you a warm welcome, introduce them to your axe and their attitude will soon change. Photo: Stevenage Museum

Heading North

Those spurning the civilised delights of the long-conquered south may have your eye on the opportunities offered by the north. In this case, the likelihood is that they you will pass through the area of the Six Hills.

If you're here in the early years, try a short detour to Lobe Hill, which is by Box Wood. There you can see a traditional small farming community getting by in their traditional way, before Roman improvements start to quickly become part of the picture. Those round huts will look somewhat familiar to an honest barbarian eye. Those short of cash might also ask around to see if there's seasonal work going. These farms need their manpower during the harvest season, particularly if it looks like foul weather's coming. A ruined harvest means starvation here as much as it does back home: Rome and later Constantinople might have free grain doles, but there are no hand outs for hungry mouths here just to keep a city mob happy.

Experienced country dwellers will also spot that the locals in the British countryside follow the Gallic custom of using marl, a mineral-rich clay, as a fertiliser. It's a peculiar practice but it seems to work. We have yet to see any of the Gauls' grain harvesters though – carts with cutting combs mounted on them, pushed (not pulled) by oxen.

Notes for out-of-season travellers

Stevenage itself was not a settlement of any significance during the Roman period (it being of Saxon foundation), though the area did have scattered presence which is represented in the town's museum. The museum is underneath a church just off the town centre, from where it is signposted to visitors. Car parking is recommended at St George's Way opposite. It's open Wednesday to Friday 10-4.30, and Saturday 10-5. More details are on the website at http://www.stevenage.gov.uk/about-stevenage/museum/

The South

Camulodunum of course is a must-see. It's long been an important location. As the centre of one of the great Celtic kingdoms, Claudius made sure it had a fort planted smack in the heart of it. Several years later, the area becomes the new province's formal administrative capital, and the settlement of retired veterans in the colony makes it the heart of Little Rome. The finest nick-nacks of the empire can be had here, including the best Samian bowls. The awe-inspiring grandeur of the Temple to the Imperial Cult (Claudius in particular) stands out as the symbol of the conquest and the umbilical cord to the imperial capital. But there's also a theatre and a council building.

It also makes for a superbly impressive bonfire come the great revolt. The temple is the focus of local outrage, but also unhappily the place to which surviving local residents (who have unwisely knocked down the old legionary walls) have fled.

Come after those times and it may no longer be the seat of government, but it's a major cultural centre. The city houses Britain's only circus for starters (at least the only one we've ever seen), so if it's racing you're after with the finest four horse chariots on offer, this is your town.

Verulamium was the third city to be plundered by the Boudiccan revolt. But it soon recovers, as you'll find from the exquisite marble-effect wall plaster paintwork, and by some rather fine mosaics. The basilica looms over the town and provides a good orienteering point as you tour it. The forum contains most of what you'll need for your daily requirements, but the main draw is the theatre. It doesn't have the imposing scale you'd get in, say, Ephesus, or the backdrop of a volcano you can find at Tauromenum in Sicily. It's plainer than Aurasio's over in Gaul. But it has one major thing going for it: it's here.

Fishbourne is a palatial villa you're unlikely to get an invite to, which is a shame as you'll miss its sumptuous echoes of the Italian ruling class, and its luxuriously scaled mosaics. Its gardens alone stand out as a residence of taste. But there are three towns from Cogidubnus's client kingdom that you can much more freely explore. Noviomagus Reginorum (Chichester) is the largest conurbation in the area. As such it has a sufficient market place for your needs and its bath house will help you unwind after a day's travelling. Note the slightly unusual flint walls if you're visiting in the later seasons, giving it a little bit of a unique flavour just as the wealthy start to move in and larger buildings get built. If you're thinking of coming at the walls in numbers, you might also want to note the defensive towers that are going up to as these could have artillery mounted on them, giving the defenders a bit of added pep from a distance, so don't make yourself too noticeable as a prime target. A softer touch would be one of the plush villas also being developed. The one at Bignor we are told has such a selection of remarkable mosaics (including one of Venus and cherub gladiators) that there must be moveable treasures to set them off, and which can also be carted off.

Calleva Atrebatum (Silchester) developed from an iron age town originally, and lies on the main road connecting Londinium with the south west so you may find it a useful travelling stop. Note that wide loads will need to enter or leave via the east or western gates, as the other roads are funnelled through narrower gateways. The forum basilica is obviously in the town centre, but you'll find the baths to the south east, and entertainment in the form of an amphitheatre lies a short walk outside the town to the east (try nipping through the small gate nearby if it's been opened for the locals). It's compact, but you can still expect on a plum fight day to see several thousand people squeezed into the space. Nip outside during a quiet moment and have a browse at the trinket stalls outside selling curios and mementos of your visit. Check with the town announcer before coming as on some days they have special events such as horse displays. As you'd expect there are a number of small temples and plenty of workshops if you are after textiles, wood, leather or metal work. Drop by Tebicatus's place by Insula IX and tell him we sent you.

The town defences will get a major work over around AD 270 and become more imposing, being raised from greenstone and limestone blocks brought in from some distance rather than local brickwork. Plan ahead. You'll need a ladder at least three men high to get over. Late travellers should also bear in mind that as the Saxons take over the places to the east the gate facing Londinium gets sealed up. It's a hindrance if you try to ride through it, an obstruction if you were planning to ram and charge through it, but more significantly a huge symbol of what's happened to the country, and the divisions now across it.

Venta Belgarum (Winchester) has a temple to the matres or mother goddesses of Britain and several other provinces (see our section on religion). While it's one of the top half a dozen towns in Britain it's not really a major tourist stop, though you'll find its position on the trade road and by a navigable river does mean that you can find buyers and sellers for your material here. Have a look at the New Forest Ware pottery in particular which is of nearby manufacture, typically of a red or dull purple colour and sometimes with simple additional paintwork decoration. The kilns are unusual and resemble more the kind of manufacturing that takes place nearer our own borders, so if you are visiting bring a sample or two along and see if there's a local taste for some of your homespun pottery for your next visit. Its importance will drop in the fourth century so come before then.

Durnovaria (Dorchester) is a more unusual place. Start just outside of town with the imposing and huge ditches and ramparts of what some call Maiden Castle. This is a settlement that predates the Romans, and since hill forts are these days considered far too aery for civilised life, you'll find the site largely undulating fields these days. Surprisingly though if you come here in the late fourth century you'll spot a small temple complex. One person we spoke to suggested it was appropriate atonement for Vespasian when he took the fort three centuries before, though the priest was out when we tried to find out more about the nearby circular shrine.

Durnovaria itself you can see from the ramparts, including the aqueduct that supplies the settlement with its fresh water. Strain your eyes to the nearer outskirts and you may spot another old Celtic fieldwork, now used as the town's amphitheatre.

Retrace your steps and head into town. As you enter, you'll pass by a number of town houses. If you can manage to get yourself invited to nip into one for a quick tour, note the flint walls, central heating, and widespread use of mosaics on the floors (they're very fond of red, black, white and yellow). There are reasonable quality craftsmen available locally, and even if some of the work can look a little clunky, there's nothing to compare with it back home. Much the same can be said of the artists. They aren't a patch on anything the Italians have to offer, but looking at the faces painted onto the walls of a local tomb and it can almost distract you from the serious business of grave-robbing.

Even here in these smaller houses you can find little ornate column pillars propping up frontages, adding both a rustic charm and a sense of discrete civilisation. But move on to the city centre. Aim for the marketplace where you'll find a good cross-selection of pottery, and get some idea of the trading opportunities that come from the local quarries.

Caesaromagus (Chelmsford)

The mansio dominates the small town of Caesaromagus, called by some Chelmsford. This is a prime stopover if you are leaving Londinium for the Camulodunum run, coming just after the main river crossings just over halfway on the route. If you are on official business, then you'll be staying in a lot of these as you make your way up and down the road system. You can already get a feel for the luxury accommodation that a person with connections can enjoy during your travels.

The mansio is an official building which combines three functions – a communications centre, a resting stop, and the local town hall. Stable your horses, and yourself, overnight here and move on to the next mansio a day's trip down the road. It lies within its own precinct within the town, and is almost self-sufficient. The adjacent bath house is certainly conveniently sited. If you hang around late enough, an octagonal fourth century temple lies a short walk away. Leave a gift to the gods attached to the sacred pole.

A villa in the countryside is usually the business heart of a large agricultural estate. If you are after plunder, this is the place to start.
Picture by Frank Gardiner copyright Essex County Council

Notes for out-of-season travellers
Finds from the excavations are on display at Chelmsford Museum, Oaklands Park, Moulsham Street, Chelmsford, Essex, CM2 9AQ (01245 605700). The most up-to-date details are on www.chelmsford.gov.uk/museums, but admission is free, and current opening hours are Mondays-Saturdays 10-5 and Sundays 1-4, but closed Fridays in school term time.
Note that the comedy series Chelmsford 123, set in ancient Caesaromagus, should be taken with a pinch of salt. As should anyone calling themselves Badvoc.

Rockbourne Villa

Rockbourne's a working villa more to the south west of Londinium, so if you're coming up from the south coast it'll make a welcome stopover for you. It's got bath houses, underfloor heating, and as its a working estate there are workshops if you need any repairs doing on any of your wagons if you've hired some. They may not be the finest in the empire, but look beyond the individual the slightly clunky red, white and black tiles, and the mosaics do add a real touch of class to the rooms. Depending on when you visit, you might find yourself allowed free run of just one of the wings while the other is still lived in by the family. But with forty rooms across the compound, even if you only get to use a couple you'll still get to feel like a senator for a day.

The other big plus with staying at this site is the space. Often villas are formally laid out with set wings and structures; here, they have the west range (next to where the old cottage used to be) with the west baths sitting inside it (get your water from the well outdoors just beside them); then there's the east baths; then the farm buildings stretch out along the southern range. But the gaps between break the claustrophobia. It helps being beside the woods and able to go for a stroll amongst the hazels, pine and silver birch. Or you can stick right up close to the villa and cheekily pick the odd cherry or plum for a succulent snack.

The richer locals have rebuilt their farms in Roman style. You will find plenty to make an attack worthwhile.
Picture by Mike Codd copyright Rockbourne Villa/Hampshire County Council.

In the third century, drop by the nearby kilns and pick up a souvenir pot to remember your stay. Steer your feet also by the corn driers and discuss with the workers your respective tips on brewing. Celtic beer is definitely something you should become acquainted with during your stay – far better quality than the dishwater beer they make over in Egypt.

Those thinking of hanging around and the type of people who keep putting business trips off might want to reconsider and look at the last illustration in the book, which shows the site after its glory days are gone. Best to reflect upon what timings best suit your diaries after all.

> **Notes for out-of-season travellers**
> Rockbourne sits around ten miles from Salisbury, and full details on how to get there can be found on the website at http://www3.hants.gov.uk/rockbourne-roman-villa.htm.
> Much of the site has been covered over to protect it, but the best bits have been left exposed.
> There's a small associated museum, and it's open from April through to the end of September, Thursdays, Fridays, Sundays and Bank Holiday Mondays between 11 and 4. There may be some changes in the new season so, as with all museum details provided, do check on the website before visiting. The postcode is SP6 3PG for your satnav.
> The artist is Mike Codd, who also contributed a number of pictures to the evocative Rockbourne guide – one of the best presented and attractive guidebooks we've seen, and we hope both in print and available in the museum.

Vectis (Isle of Wight)

As you travel around the south coast of Britain, you may find yourself passing through the area of the natural harbours known as Magnus Portus. If you are in Noviomagus Reginorum, an old military supply harbour nearby gives you an equally good opportunity. Whatever occasion presents, take a local vessel and dart across the narrow waters that separate the mainland from this island. You're following in the path of Vespasian, who conquered this tract. You're also at hub of imperial politics for a short while in AD 296, when Allectus's admirals await with their gathered ships to do battle with the invasion fleet of Constantius. Fog stops play for them, preventing a mighty naval battle, but doesn't halt the invasion. If you are in the area during this season, the dinner parties have a high note of drama and considerable tension to them. If you come later, look out from the veranda on a murky day and try to imagine the fleet commanders peering through the gloom as their doom silently passes them by. Or imagine the sight from the north of the island as patches of fog lift, and the stench and sight of vast columns of smoke and spluttering flames rise from the opposite shore as the landing army burns its own ships before pressing on with its invasion. It truly is a terrible harbinger of doom.

Of the five or so villas on the island, we recommend you stop off at welcoming Newport. It's a late farmhouse built around AD 280. The design is quite marked. Look up outside at what look like gnarly tree growths. These are in fact three plastered domes. These are made out of tufa, a strange rock that's light and holey, that the Romans charmingly call 'cats' brains'. These domes allowed the condensed steam in the three heated rooms to run down the walls rather than drip onto the bathers below.

As you're heading around the island, you'll quickly see that agriculture holds sway in the south. Beyond the ridge that cuts the island in two, the north is more rugged and wooded. If you happen to be travelling late and looking for a place to crash, avoid buildings like the one above. This is a typical corn drier, and quite apart from the lack of comfort, the smell and the confined space, being found by an angry farmer the next day in a room that can be fired up but only has a single exit is not a healthy predicament. If trapped, break out through the roof. Don't bother stealing any tools for selling on your trade travels. The Romans introduce the scythe beyond

Back home a stone house like this would be home to a rich man. Don't be fooled. The Britons use them to dry grain. Copyright Isle of Wight Heritage Service.

Hadrian's Wall, but it falls out of use again locally when they withdraw south again.

The straits dividing the island from the mainland are narrow, but strongly tidal. Note that there's a Saxon Shore fort at the west of the island, and that the hills provide a reasonable view to the south. We suggest to raiders you try your chances with a speedy rush in straight from the south east.

> **Notes for out-of-season travellers**
> Newport Roman Villa has one of the country's best preserved Roman bath suites. It's open through 8 April to end October, 10.30 to 4 Mondays to Saturdays and Sundays in July and August 12-4. It's located at Cypress Road, Newport on the Isle of Wight (PO30 1HE). The site was only occupied for around half a century so it provides a fairly straightforward layout to understand, and also hosts a reconstructed period kitchen and garden. For more details, look under Museums in the Places to Go section of the Council website, http://www.iow.gov.uk/homepage/, which also has details on the nearby villa at Brading with its important and remarkable mosaics.

The West and South West

Where the west begins is a matter of opinion, at least until a provincial capital is carved out to run it. We start our tour with Corinium (Cirencester). Originally a small settlement beside a nondescript fortlet, it's grown by Hadrian's time to over 10,000 people, giving Londinium a run for its money, and is large enough to draw Hadrian during his visit. With its impressive amphitheatre (which you can find in in a small quarter just outside of town), its quality buildings and major market, it runs a close second to Londinium. Corinium is a handy spot to base yourself if you are in the area for villa-spotting, since there are a number of imposing and important ones nearby, as well as some important temple sites in the neighbouring countryside.

If Corinium has a competitor ultimately it's Viroconium

Cornoviorum (Wroxeter). Viroconium is much further up to the north, essentially on the tip of what's the west and the middle lands, and it's this siting which leads to it becoming one of the provincial capitals in later years. If you're doing business in the third century onwards, chances are some contracts will draw you here. The bath house is so solid and elephantine you could imagine huge chunks of it could last a thousand years or more. Drop by the upmarket forum for the choicest samian bowls or mortaria, the gritty kitchen bowls. In bad weather drop by the macellum or indoor market and do your buying under cover, especially if it's foodstuffs you're after. Those in need of some moral guidance can drop in opposite at the large temple – the entrance is where the six exotic columns stand, all in the Corinthian style and looking at the top like they've turned into plant fronds. After admiring the statues inside, later visitors should turn now to watch the garrison practise throwing their large darts: it might be useful judging the distances you may need to keep between you and any chasing sentries if you have any late night skullduggery in mind. Darts replace the heavy throwing spears of earlier years, so if in the dark you hear one whizz by your head, you know to beware as they are small enough for the soldier to have a couple more stashed to hand. Bear this town in mind if you're a very late season visitor. Though you'll find the worn basilica torn down, the ruler's put up some timber residences instead, in which you can meet and hear tales of old Rome. Indeed, the west and the north are your best spots to find it clinging on.

If the north is your stomping ground, it's likely your route at some point will take you through Letocetum given that it's near a major crossroads. It also happens to be on an old tribal border, and in many ways marks out the edge of the west and the boundary with the north. There's a quality mansio here of course, and a decent set of baths, at least until a spot of local difficulties at the end of the second century during which time you'd be advised to take a leave of absence. Other than that it's a fair stopping point but hardly a thrusting cosmopolis.

Aquae Sulis (Bath) is a must-see town for travellers in these parts. Its fame comes from its waters, and while the layout of the town as it nestles by a river in amongst the hills is appealing (especially given the glow of the local stone), you've really come to visit the sacred spring. Hot water gushes out of the rock, and is channelled into a special baths complex for visitors to make use of it. Tasting it isn't much fun (it has a pungent bitterness a little bit like toasted leggings), so if you're not up for that, hold your nose and bathe in it instead. If, on the other hand, you have some business dealings that have gone wrong lately, join a queue and write out a curse on a lead tablet, fold it up, and throw it in the watery pit to descend directly to the gods of the underworld. A local angry person will probably be delighted to show you how to fill in one of these defixiones, if you can endure a short rant on how he's been short-changed himself. While you are here, drop by the temple as well, which is one of only a couple that have been built in the province in the traditional classical style. Marvel in particular at the carved gorgon's head. You'll spot it prominently set in the centre of the structure, and looks like a face surrounded by hair after being struck by lightning.

We move now to the south western tip of the island. Those who live in the area of the promontory called Belerium have a reputation of being particularly welcoming to strangers, and you may seek to come here in particular. Their long trade in tin has made them a particularly open society, even in pre-Roman times. In the past, tin was quarried in seams, then melted down to remove impurities and broken down into fragments the size of knuckle bones. Then, using wicker containers covered in hides, it was famously carted or 'coracled' over to an island called Ictis, a strange place since part of the time the sea recedes and it is joined to the mainland. From Ictis, it has long been exported on across to Gaul and even on down to the Rhone, though these days the ingots are far heftier blocks.

Heading instead west from Corinium takes us over the great estuary into a land of valleys and rugged hills. The Roman fortress of Isca, or as some may call it Caerleon, was set up after the civil war period to secure the area around the Usk river, and pivoted on the important waterway of the large channel that cuts into this part of the country. Make sure you get your Isca's right, because there's another one (Isca Dumnonionum) in the south west peninsular of Britain.

Venta Silurum (Caerwent) is definitely worth a diversion, and is less than a day's travel away. It used to be a very important tribal centre, which helps to explain why it has a legion camped in it. The inevitable forum and basilica in the centre aside, you can find the public bath house just off. The amphitheatre sits north east from the forum as if dropped on the neat layout by the gods from above. Don't expect too much extravagance here, as mosaics and even heating are few and far between. But do have a wander around the stylistically varied temples. To some people it's a bit of a backwater, although it's not as poor and down-to-heel as some people make out. But all the more for that there's something of a taste of the old frontier about these sturdy walls, which you suspect may outlast some of their fancier counterparts out east.

If it's real edge-of-empire and edge-of-the-world experience that you want, leave this behind and trek on north west. Segontium (near what some style Caernafon) is an auxiliary outpost right on the edge of civilisation – in fact, given how sparsely populated the far west is, some say it's the outpost's outpost. It guards the straits with the island that faces Hibernia. Other than a temple to Mithras, there's not much to see here.

The shape of civilisation changes considerably if you come

to this area out of season. While the east fills up with all manner of uncouth Saxons and such like, the west makes a play at continuing to hold together something of past glories. We recommend two destinations during this period. The first is by South Cadbury and is somewhat retro, because it's a reused hill fort from olden days. Persist with the climb. On top of the hill there's a large feasting hall. Time your arrival (and make diplomatic amends for the attitudes of your relatives) and you may be allowed a glimpse of reflected Rome. Alternatively, stick with your ship and take it and your merchant's wares round to Tintagel. Perched on an imposing peninsular on the rocky shores, this important trading centre is still dealing with what's left of the Roman world. If it's byzantine goods you're after, head for here and ask for Artognou mentioning this book. You might find him at one of buildings lower down the hillside flank.

Glevum (Gloucester)

Glevum is a one of those towns that grew up from a military background. It's a leading fortress that became a colony. An early visit here will find soldiers busy with the move from the settled quarters at Camulodunum, and for around a decade and a half this will be a major military centre for the imperial front line. Then they'll move on again to Isca, and the settlement will become a site for retired soldiers at the close of the century.

The legionary headquarters will go but the place still keeps a lot of the old army feel to it, at least for a generation or so as trusted old army types engage in much of the contract work.

These original military-style buildings won't last forever and the place gradually gets a more civilian flavour to it, though construction standards will be -shall we say - mixed. Note then that the following two centuries will see work done on the towers then the ramparts, so it's not a soft touch for raiders. If trade's your draw, there's a major brick works, and

Roman ports are packed with valuable goods, but don't try to steal anything as the army is usually on guard.
Copyright Gloucester Museums Service

the city makes its own distinctive pottery for a couple of centuries before shifting to a more farming-orientated economy. It's the furthest port from the sea so make use of any boats you may have access to. If staying here in a rainy period, watch out for flooding if you are housed on the ground floor.

If as a tourist you can see these views you are, of course, in serious trouble.

Notes for out-of-season travellers

Those looking for some general background could begin with a visit to the town's historical website, http://www.livinggloucester.co.uk. The place to visit, however, is Gloucester City Museum and Art Gallery. It's on Brunswick Road (GL1 1HP). At the time of writing it had been undergoing a major revamp and was set to reopen; we suggest you get more details on the new opening hours off the leisure and culture section of the council website, www.gloucester.gov.uk, or consider telephoning direct on 01452 396131.

Tim Copeland's 2011 book Roman Gloucestershire (available at bookstores) has come highly commended to us as an introduction to the Roman towns of the area and their environment, with a good selection of illustrations. It also covers Cirencester and a number of local villas.

The city of Glevum as you will find it on two very different dates. Above: The army fortress of Glevum in about ad80 when it was home to the Legio II Augusta. Not a good place for a barbarian to visit. Below: Colonia Nervia Glevensium in about ad150 by which time the place had become a civilian town. By this time it was home to 10,000 people and one of the biggest towns in Britain. Worth a visit, but don't cause trouble. The local militia are well trained.
Copyright Gloucester Museums Service

Badminton Villa

Glevum needn't be your only stop over if you are in the vicinity of the town. The area is noted for having a number of countryside buildings, some of quite high status.

Take in particular the villa at Badminton. From the outside the main building looks almost like a sort of church, or budget basilica, thanks to a late addition of a semi-circular extension. The whole thing's a sizeable 190 feet long, and you can already guess at the solid oak timbers keeping the roof up. But inside you'll find a spectacular mosaic, dating from around AD 370 so quite late. The munificence is set off by an apse at the far end of the room, and brightly coloured wall plaster. Go over there and, if it's put out, lounge out on the stibadium or semi-circular couch and take the opulence in over some chilled wine.

Try not to burn the place down when you leave.

The basilica at Badminton is a great place to take a rest and enjoy some of the local wine.

Notes for out-of-season travellers

The villa remains today lie in a private estate that's lived in. While the main building may be recognisable as where the pilots park their fighter planes in the Battle of Britain scene in the film Pearl Harbor, as an occupied place of residence it is not however open to the public, and access to the archaeological site is not allowed – it has been covered up again in any event. Moreover, there were few finds from the excavations other than old demolition material, so nothing to ask to see.

On the other hand, those interested in local Roman life may care to note that the nearby villa of Great Witcombe is open to the public, and details can be found on it at the English Heritage website. Many of the finds from the area can be found in Bristol Museum, which is also where you can also get a key from to visit the neighbouring Kings Weston villa and mosaics. More details via http://www.bristol.gov.uk/ under 'Leisure and Culture'.

Big stones

You're a barbarian. What do you want with old stones? They're too big for ballast and you have plenty of rubble at home.

If you are still taken by the old things from before Roman times though, there are plenty of places scattered around the countryside where large rocks have been jammed in the earth. There's little beyond local legends to say what they were there for, but to guess from our own experience they probably involved bad things happening to people to stop more bad things happening to everyone. But who's to say?

If proto-sculpture is your thing, head for the plains in the south west where there are huge stones with lids on. Nearby there's a massive mound the size of a hill, made by man. We suspect it covers a huge tomb with gold in it, though we gave up trying to dig it up after a couple of days' pointless labour when the locals chased us away with farming implements. It is also said that some of the islands in the lands of the Picts, in the far North and North West, have impressive stones and works rendered beautiful by their scale and nature-wracked surroundings. These spots are well known to locals wherever you are in the country, and may provide some distraction if you are looking for an alternative day out. We recommend you leave your shovel at home, however.

Lindum and the East

Just as Corinium gets picked to run the western of the two new provinces with the fourth century reforms, the eastern portion falls to a new capital at Lindum. It's not just our own connections with this part of the world which lead us to recommend a visit. At the close of the first century, it was one of only four cities in Britain to be designated as a colonia, a top notch provincial urban centre. The area has had mixed fortunes over the years. The arrival of the Romans saw some major work done on reclaiming land from the sea. Some of that work was undone in the late third century during a time of troubles, and things have gotten worse since. But away from the flat lands, in places such as the valley of the river Nene, for instance, you can find a pottery industry conveniently sited on the east coast which you may wish to explore developing trade contacts with. They make a wide selection of products from a quite durable material, ranging from jugs to bottles, dishes and beakers. Colours vary significantly, with dark grey not uncommon but not unique – you can even find some imitation posh samian, and can request hunting or religious scenes as extras. It's sold all over the island, and at first sight looks a little like the equivalents from the lower Rhine. Later trade approaching the low season is more of the coarse wear type but still popular. We recommend it highly as a reasonably priced gift table set.

Lindum itself offers an imposing first sight to visitors, perched as it is on a hill. It's another case of a town that developed once the original legion moved on to catch up with the new frontier. Ignore the condition of the early walls as you go in, which may be of stone but are also leaning a bit thanks to a lack of serious foundations. One thing you certainly won't sniff at is the sewerage system, which is superb. Look for the main buildings at the top of the hill, as the commercial side of things is lower down, particularly where it runs into the outskirts where the old native settlement stood. There are baths despite the hill – they're fed by a water tank. Private residences are more on the outskirts, particularly by the mid-season. Shopping, we suggest tracking down the brooch makers who are highly inventive; we stocked up on some wonderful fun ones that looked like roosters and hares.

As an excursion, we suggest catching a ride on one of the riverine boats that ply the area. Ask by the lower southern gate to see what cargo boats are doing that day. Take a packed lunch and get off after an hour or so for a gentle stroll back. Alternatively, simply walk down to the bridge for a fish's eye view of the colonia looming above. If you have any administrative difficulties, we found local councillor Aurelius Senecio to be a useful man to know.

This part of the island isn't densely populated, but amongst the places of interest in its idyllic countryside you might find yourself making a short stop off at Lactodurum (Towcester). Ask one of the outlying farmers to point out where they say Boudicca's army was smashed. The village itself has a few shops, all rather grim at the outset with timber walls and clay floors, but spruced up with stone walls and mortar floors in the second century, and some tesselated work and columns in the century following. So keep an eye open as you pass down this main road over the years and you'll see a settlement that's a microcosm of civilisation improving over time. The statue on the tomb just outside of town also merits keeping an eye open for, with its long drawn face.

Stonea Grange is a curiosity worth stopping by if you are hunting fowl in the Fens. It lies on a gravelly rise in the marshes, surrounded by imperial estate (and with some links to the old fight against the invader). The settlement here isn't massive, but it's well planned and there's a large stone edifice at its heart. It won't last long doing its administrative function, closing down in the late second century, but if you visit during this time it's a strange sight, seeing it rise out of the marsh, that reminds you of what the poets say about the Romans bringing order and civilisation to barbarian chaos. Follow the track also to the nearby temple complex for a refreshing walk.

Travelling to Venta Icenorum (Caistor) takes you across either the Fens or the Wash if you coming from Lindum. The road network itself coming up from Londinium drives through Camulodunum, meaning that geographically Venta is in the East, but for road traffic it's long been linked with the south. That isolation is useful if you are planning on direct travel from home with a raiding party. It's old Iceni territory of course. Look out for the strange 'Y' building.

Ratae Corieltauvorum (Leicester)

The Romans found a few huts and made of it a military camp, which in time has become a city. That is the story of Ratae. Ratae's an important stop on the route up north, and at a significant river crossing. Yet despite that it's going to take a good fifty years before people start putting up decent stone buildings.

Still, those improvements do come and the place starts to turn into a more upheel town. When wall paintings go up there's some effort put into the design. A temple to Jupiter gets built. And in around AD 125 up go our favourite site, the baths – or rather that's when the work starts because, as a hefty building put up through local taxes, it'll take a while before it's properly finished. Admire its chunky glass windows.

That also of course meant an aqueduct had to be built too. So fresh water now comes into town in streams. It's not enough to put out the fire that hits the place around AD 360, so time your visit to come before then as the great buildings in the town, including the forum and the basilica as well as the baths, won't get rebuilt. That's a shame, as the macellum or market place is an impressive fifty feet high.

One of Ratae's local heroes is Marcus Ulpius Novantico. During the wars in Dacia under Trajan, he and his colleagues in a cohort of Britons are given accelerated Roman citizenship on account of their service. Novantico's a soldier whose one of them, and you may bump into his proud father, Adcobrovatus.

Notes for out-of-season travellers

If you like your archaeology to be chunky and still standing, Leicester has a large slab of Roman wall just for you. The nearby museum which contains the council's Roman Leicester collections is Jewry Wall Museum, St Nicholas Circle, Leicester, LE1 4LB. Note that there is no on-site parking, though the site is about ten minutes walk from the city centre.

For details on visits and opening times, the telephone number is 0116 225 4971, and the website http://www.leicester.gov.uk/museumsandgalleries which includes advice on getting there. The museum is open 11.00-4.30 February to October.

Those seeking more on ancient Leicester might profitably look up the local archaeological unit's publication Visions of Ancient Leicester, published by the University and again featuring work by the excellent Mike Codd, and is available both locally and online through http://shop.le.ac.uk/.

Piddington

Travelling to the north and reaching the area around the village of Bannaventa? If you're in no hurry, turn off Watling Street and head for the nearby villa of Tiberius Claudius Verus. It may be slightly off the beaten track, but don't let that put you off, especially as there is a good minor road network of tracks to local settlements such as Duston and Irchester, and the promise of dinner invites to other local villas.

His family have been living here for as long as anyone can

remember. Indeed, he points out his ancestors had to put up with a Roman military camp slap on their doorstep for a couple of years when the frontier advanced through here. The old round houses obviously are long gone now, and the first villa may have been a little plain and rural, but its successor building has since grown in size and style as two and then three wings were added. Both Verus and his successor, Tiberius Claudius Severus, take real pride in the place.

The wall paintings include cinnabar, brought over from Asia Minor. After you've taken the time to look over the detailed mosaic in the dining room, go and admire the stone-lined well, quite probably the deepest you'll see anywhere on these islands, as wide as a man with arms outstretched, and excellent for fresh chilled water on a hot day. The walled inner gardens make for a pleasant morning stroll. Over the wall in the distance you can just make out the local iron works, where you can get repairs made to travelling utensils. Ask the owner before he takes his small dog for a walk around the estate if he'll show you his small clasp knife, a unique and wonderful little figure of a secutor gladiator. While he's out, nip down to the cool cellar for a strange view through the shuttered windows set at ground level, looking out through the bushes into the front garden and the gravel walkway. Mind the friendly mice, and avoid the temptation to drink too obvious an amount of the stockpiled beverages down there.

Sadly the heyday of Severus's villa in the second century won't last. We weren't around for it but we gather his descendant picks the wrong side during some political troubles. The later occupants make do with taking over just a few rooms to run the farm as the place slowly falls down around them - a foretaste of the fate of all villas a century later. Still, the last occupants are Saxons, so late visitors should have little need for interpreters when looking for a quiet, if increasingly slum-quality, place to hole up for the evening when passing through.

> ## Notes for out-of-season travellers
> The Piddington site is on private land, excavated by the Upper Nene Archaeological Society (UNAS), predominantly through an annual dig every August which has been taking place for a third of a century. As a volunteer organisation it is extremely friendly and open to potential new members who may be interested in trying their hand at excavating for the first time.
>
> The finds from the site are displayed at a small museum in the adjacent village. It's not a huge collection but the finds and reconstruction work are well presented. It's open on Sunday afternoons, 2-4 over October to March, and 2-5 over April to end September. Details on UNAS and the museum can be found on http://www.unas.org.uk/, telephone: 01604 870312/871266, or email piddington.museum@tiscali.co.uk. You can also find out more about open days where the site itself might be viewed and explained, perhaps with other events also set up for visitors.

The Saxon Shore Forts

Stretching out from Dubris all the way to the fringes of the north, eyes will be on you. The Romans aren't too keen on raiders, and to hinder your more militant forays into tourism there is a range of towers and small forts keeping watch over illicit landings.

They're called Saxon Shore forts as they're there to stop the land they're on becoming Saxon. And then when the settlement of Saxon mercenaries takes place, that makes the name twice as relevant.

Strictly speaking the ones at the far ends of the chain aren't Saxon Shore forts at all. They're old style forts and ports. Some of the harbours in the south we've already mentioned are merely extensions of the chain. But however you want to classify it, if you come across one the effect is still going be the same. A warning message will travel at the speed of light, meaning as fast as it takes for one tower to spot someone has lit a flame. From then on the clock is dripping (it's a water clock, remember).

Regulbium or Reculver gives us an example of the sort of

place we're talking about, though it could be one of a dozen others. It's originally a first century fort but gets enlarged when the others to the north get built. It lies about three quarters of a mile from the coast (though mind the cliff face as it's receding). Othona (Bradwell-on-Sea) may well also be worth a visit, and during a very late out-of-season trip we overheard a monk talking of putting up a Saxon chapel there, and it sounded very impressive and all rather symbolic of how things had turned around.

Scarborough Signal Station

Built in the later fourth century, this fortified watchtower won't be an easy place to crash and burn. It's a good ninety feet high and solid with it, but also surrounded with sturdy walls designed to keep out the casual attacker - at least long enough for the message to get out that there are unwelcome visitors approaching the shore.

It's not a place to love. It looks almost industrial once the flames are going, a little perhaps like a crematorium of a harsh and cruel king. But it's not meant to be admired: its purpose is to watch over the seas and pass a message, and that message is that you are coming.

With observation posts such as these dotted along the eastern coast, raiders will feel the need for speed. On the other hand, if you're clearly in a trading vessel and having some difficulties in a storm, you may find that they are a lifesaver in spreading the word that you're foundering, and there are people to be wrenched from the crashing shoreline waves.

Notes for out-of-season travellers

The signal station stood on a site now occupied by the castle. The painting shown above was commissioned for the Rotunda Museum. The Museum, which is by the Grand Hotel, is open 10-5 Tuesdays to Sundays plus Bank Holidays, and you can get the latest details to help plan a visit on its website at http://www.scarboroughmuseumstrust.org.uk/. We recommend the William Street car park. While hardly a Roman, we definitely suggest you see if Gristhorpe Man is on display – a bronze age chief who was buried inside a hollowed-out log.

The signal station itself is marked out by a ditch and outline at an English Heritage site up on the cliffs, though it was itself superceded by later chapels whose foundations are more obvious relics. You can get there by heading up Castle Road. Check the English Heritage website for opening times in advance as it's not open all year round.

The artist, Heather Elvidge, can be contacted on elvidge@muston.eclipse.co.uk

Eboracum and the North

You can't come all the way to Britain and not see it. Eboracum is the northernmost jewel of Roman civilisation, reportedly two hundred and twenty seven thousand paces from Londinium (we recommend you don't try counting them). It's the city of emperors. It's a key part of the northern military complex (so steer clear of trying to assault it). And it's got all the touches of Rome you could seek.

Its waterfront facilities and demanding population (including grouchy soldiers) means that it's the emporium of the north. Look in the shops for engraved glassware or fine lamps by Fortis. There are local potteries and tile manufacturers if army surplus material is what you're after. The city is a major manufacturer of jet carvings, a German frontier favourite, so fans of this black stone should definitely stock up during the visit.

The city is divided into two by the river Ouse. It's a pleasant enough stream to follow; tip Marcus Minucius Audens a couple of coins and he may take you along on a short trip next time he acts as a pilot. Ask him for a couple of stories from his military service to pass the hours. If you're there at the end of the first century, see if you can drop by the bar when Demetrius of Tarsus is there. Demetrius explored some of the islands of Britain for Vespasian. Later on you might try to drop by Marcus Aurelius Lunaris, a handy man to know for all his contacts, as he trades with the main city of south western Gaul and is also a priest of the imperial cult both here and in Lindum.

Keep to the south west of the river unless you have a reason to be in the military quarter, especially if there's trouble on the frontier. The military area itself is huge, a good fifty acres. It's long needed to be, since the place has long housed the best part of a full legion. Look at Constantine's walls as you approach from the south, and you'll be impressed by the formidable broad towers. It's also the quarter with the greatest historical pull, with the headquarters associated with every emperor whose ever come up to campaign on the empire's borders, supported by titanic pillars.

Even so, you'll be able to visit the bath house to the south of the river, one of the largest in the country, and if you're able to pull some strings you might be able to get a glimpse inside the imperial residence. It's out of use now of course, or rather a bit short of the fancy furnishings, but you can still get a tingle as you step in the tracks of great men.

If purple isn't your colour but you're still into the borderland city experience, then head south west for Deva Victrix (Chester). It's the Roman gateway onto the middle sea. Arriving by boat brings you into the harbour area with the warehouses sited to the west of the town, by the military quarter. The bustle however lies in the more densely packed eastern part of the place. Outside of the walls you get a semi-rural feel, and there's nothing so pleasant on a summer's day as strolling down to the water's edge to watch the boats go by, or listening to the strain of the sailors as they tentatively manoeuvre under the arches of the great bridge before scrambling into action to make the sharp turn as the river bends. Deva dominates the North West in the way that Eboracum looms over the mid north. Originally intended to keep the western mountains of the island under control, the fort's massive stone wall (built under Trajan) still impress. Check out the south east of the town. The area is dominated by an amphitheatre capable of seating several thousand. A fitting touch if you can spot it is the little shrine to the goddess Nemesis. It's not the biggest amphitheatre you'll come across but you might sense a different feel from it, as overwhelmingly its customers come from the barracks and the sandy part is larger than you'll be used to, designed as it is to cater for the military using it to practise. When they're not training, or executing some malfaisants on a timber scaffold, you might be able to get access and watch some blood sports alongside veterans who do the same work in the field. Perhaps you may find it makes the 'civilian' amphitheatres a little more tasteless afterwards, since the audience have little real appreciation of what the victims genuinely might be feeling.

Dismiss such thoughts and clean the dust off at the baths, from whose size alone you can tell this is a major legionary city packed full of soldiery. If you can get into the military sector, ask to see the Ellyptical Building. It's an unusually shaped large posh oval edifice with a pleasant fountain in the middle, providing a civilised refuge from the toils of the day.

Gastronauts will not be disappointed. The town has a variety of suppliers of the best sea food, reared animals, deer and boar. Goose, pheasant and swan can also be found. If the opportunity to binge gets the better of you and stomach ache strikes, track down Hermogenes the doctor to sort you out. Be patient with his Latin accent as he's a Greek speaker; a bit of pointing is probably enough.

If you're at a loose end, and you're leaving town heading south, drop by the quarry and ask to see the shrine to Minerva. It's a quirky little thing unusually cut out of the living rock.

If the country resort is your thing, explore the wild hills of the north and head for Aquae Arnemetiae (Buxton). Part of the charm of this area is that it's a backwater, many of whose residents are in fact engaged in the mining trade, particularly for lead. But the holy woods which hide these warm waters conceal a hidden gem. Its natural springs are as healthy as those of Aquae Sulis, Britannia's other spa town, but with less of the showiness and bustle.

Northwards, ever northwards, however is where you're heading if you are looking to supply the military market. Isurium Brigantum (Aldborough) is a key site perched (as the name suggests) on old Brigantes land. Look to the nearby hill for the amphitheatre with a view outside as well as in.

Before you know it, the military road has swept you up as far as Pons Aelius (Newcastle). It's an important crossing point of a significant river, hence the name of the place, recalling Hadrian's work. The bridge that does the job is a sturdy piece of engineering, as the multiple arches suggest. As you cross, see if the altars to Neptune and to Oceanus are still there on either side. We thoroughly recommend if you're leaving the empire to stop over at route at Corstopitum or colloquially Coria (Corbridge), which has the unique claim of being the empire's northernmost settlement, though its off-duty rowdy legionaries keep reminding you that you're far from quieter lands. You can practise your Latin on the altar stones that keep popping up under your feet, dedicated by soldiers after various deeds of derring-do to all manner of favoured military Gods whether Celtic, Roman, or Eastern like Baal.

Drop by the market for any nick nacks you're short of (forget the granaries as they are off limits), and get any last minute work on any metalware done here in town before you leave Roman territory. We recommend the excellent field anvil, basically a sturdy little square peg hammered into the turf like a tent peg as far as its stabilisers. Later visitors might look around in case anyone is selling a cento, a sort of unauthorised felt under-helmet that can be dipped in water to keep your head cool on a hot day (when they occur). A must-have is one of the bronze souvenir bowls that are on sale, bearing the names of the frontier forts in the vicinity. You can even get one commissioned with your name on it. The prettiest have enamel inlay in a flash of colours.

Alternatively, look around for Barates, a friendly Palmyran from whom you might be able to buy a surplus standard as a souvenir if you have the space in the luggage. He has some time on his hands as he's just lost his wife, a southern British woman called Regina who he points out was very good at knitting. Regina had been his slave before he freed her. But he'll be happy to while away some moments discussing what he's seen of the other end of the Roman Empire, and the journeys he's had to get here.

A must-see however before you do depart is the fountain house, which is where the water is pushed out from an aqueduct for the residents to be able to drink. It makes a refreshing place to pause on a warm day. As you leave town, give the sandstone lion eating a deer a pat for good luck. It used to be a funerary monument but has been put to new decorative use.

Travellers heading up via the west coast on the other hand will be drawn naturally towards Lugovalium (Carlisle). This has more of a real border town feel to it, a bit edgier perhaps. Given the number of auxiliaries on the frontier though you may start to feel a little more at home, and it's certainly less official 'legionary Roman' than Pons Aelius. Despite its location, you can also find Greek spoken here. Uniquely, Lugovalium is where you'll find a training centre for stone carvers, which makes sense if you consider the size of the masonry they have to maintain. You certainly have to see the impressive workmanship on the frontier defences. Hadrian's Wall is a serpent of stone stretching from sea to sea, studded with towers and forts. It's far more impressive than the turf Antonine Wall built further north. See if you can spot where Hadrian, who was clearly something of an obsessive for uniformity and going by the book, orders postern gateways to be built where - if they were ever used - soldiers would teeter on the edge of cliffs. If you ever need to cross it illicitly however, pick a windy, cold and wet day when the guards have nipped inside to put on their leggings. So long as you're quick and have a bit of rope you should be alright. The wall's been built to impress, mark and awe, to stop you dashing south and running back north again with someone's herd of cattle. There's no way you can sneak a herd back over this obstacle. And if you bought it legally, here's where you can be taxed on it.

The military frontier provides the trader with a number of opportunities for making a profit providing homely luxuries. Here is the end of all things, and the beginning. This is the boundary of Rome, where the god Terminus reigns.

Some last handy hints? Consider the following:

• The military supply chain, even on the border, reaches back a long way. Quality quern stones are brought over from the Rhineland; pottery and oysters from the south east; other pottery and grinding mortars from the south west. If it's needed, and you can supply it, you may have a market despite the distance.

• Up here, swords are made locally from ore, together with some pottery and the roofing tiles. Know your market.

• Preferred styles can vary depending on the origins of the local soldiers. There are some really weird and ugly pots being made for the more exotic garrisons. If you can supply the sort of things they are used to back home, you might make a premium.

•Note that even in the military on the frontier, fashions change, for instance in footwear styles. If you are ahead of the new styles, you might find a captive audience on the frontier.

•If travelling further north out of necessity, with a Roman unit chasing you, remember that they can put temporary horse shoes on their hooves to make them cover rough ground or even cross ice. Don't loiter!

Thorpe Thewles

Not all of Britain after the Romans' first arrival instantly looks like what we'd call Roman. Away from the main urban centres, old ways of doing things take some time to die away, giving visitors a chance to look at 'authentic' British life. That's especially the case once you get away from the 'concentrated Roman-ness' of the early south east.

Thorpe Thewles gives us one such example; even in around AD 50-100, you can drop by and get a sense of the old way of life. It helps that being this far north the Romans are taking a generation to come here. Round huts and thatched roofs – it's almost as fun as camping, or if you're a homesick barbarian a cheap way of remembering life back home. It won't last this old iron age lifestyle, so enjoy it while you can.

Nearby Catcote gives an example of how this 'style creep' takes place. At first, before the Romans get this far there's a little trade and no oblong buildings. Then, with the Conquest, rectangular buildings start to be built, often by the wealthier people such as the local chief who is trying to impress his fellows. A lot of pottery and glass from down south comes in. With a nearby beach handily acting as a spot for transshipment, the village increases in importance, and with it the taste for the trends of stranger parts. Oblong is in.

The following shows the sort of small rural settlement you're likely to come across in this early era of Romanisation.

The village of Thorp Thewles shows you what Britain was like before the Romans came. And a jolly good place to grab some stew and beer Illustration by Andrew Hutchinson, (c) Tees Archaeology.

Notes for out-of-season travellers

There's nothing much today to see at the site itself, but finds from Thorpe Thewles are on display at Preston Hall Museum in Preston Park (TS18 3RH), albeit thematically rather than set out together showing the site. The museum has been undergoing refurbishment, so visitors are advised to get the latest details from the Stockton council site, http://www.stockton.gov.uk. Catcote's finds on the other hand are in the Museum of Hartlepool (situated by the marina).

More information on the work undertaken by Tees Archaeology is set out on their website, http://www.teesarchaeology.com/, including the latest digital newsletter that's useful if you are a local, or seeking to volunteer some free digging time.

The artist Andrew Hutchinson is a countryside and wildlife illustrator, more of whose work and contact details can be found at www.illustrationweb.com/artists/AndrewHutchinson. He exhibits locally at the Stacy-Marks Gallery (Helmsley) and The Artsbank (Saltburn) as well as holding an annual one day exhibition at Sunnyfield House, Westgate, Guisborough each November (see local press nearer the time for dates).

Vindolanda

Until you've seen a Roman fort, up close or even at a distance, you won't get the healthy respect you need for taking on the Roman army. So for much of the Roman period, you really do need to travel up to the frontier to get the feel.

Vindolanda is an excellent place to pick. It's a pretty major fort some way along the wall, nestling in a valley just a couple of miles behind the patrolling sentries, so you get a flavour of genuine frontier life rather than something more 'towny'. Try not to stare as you approach if they've mounted a trophy skull on the wall as a message to troublemakers. Aim for the vicus, or neighbouring civilian settlement, as the place to lay your head.

If you get on well with any of the senior staff, and they trust you, don't be surprised if they hand you a small packet when you leave. It'll be a small letter written on wood, and it's for handing over when you pass through some destination. They are real scribblers here, whether its gossip, or invites to parties, or business dealings. You might find it a good opportunity to practise your own written Latin here, though getting to grips with some of the spidery scrawl can be rather tricky. Pick a sensible moment though. Marcus Aurelius Modestus might have the ear of the local commander, but he still has duties to perform. Take time out to drop by the Nervians, or the Tungrian auxiliaries when they're based here, some of whom you may recognise from you own time on the Roman-German border. You can spot them of course by their horse-headed standard.

There are again a lot of altars dotted around the place, to a variety of deities. Try to spot the one to Mogons, an unusual Celtic power. There are several to Vheterus, a familiar German war god for us. Even Neptune is honoured, this far from the coast.

The best time to visit, if you are after solid buildings, is in the late second century when a proper stone fort is first built.

Most army forts have a civilian vicus built outside. You won't be allowed into the fort itself, so stay in a tavern in the vicus instead.
(c) Vindolanda Trust

There are earlier wooden ones, which get abandoned for a short while when the frontier moves north to the Antonine Wall and the local garrisons get rationalised. On the other hand, such rustic surroundings are exactly what greet Hadrian when he's in the area building his wall, so maybe you could slum it in his little wooden palace with its wall paintings after he's gone inspecting!

Do consider coming down here even if you are an extremely tardy visitor. The place may have fallen into ruins – who needs a frontier force when there's no empire to defend – but the late church still juts out of the buildings' shards, and the priest can tell you a tale or two about the ghost armies of the past.

Notes for out-of-season travellers

The Roman Army Museum is a remarkable presentation of frontier military life with some powerful films and imagery displays, while the section dealing with the celebrated Vindolanda tablets creates a powerful connection with ordinary lives.

It's located at the Chesterholm Museum, Bardon Mill, Hexham (NE47 7JN), looking onto a high section of the Wall. It's open seven days a week but opening times do vary slightly across the year: full details are set out on the very thorough website www.vindolanda.com. It proved a rich site, including the largest collection of Roman leather anywhere, and spectacularly presented, while the archaeology itself is still surviving in sufficient quantity to be readily interpretable. And of course for the full experience you should drop by the recreated nymphaeum on a fine day.

Travelling Beyond the Empire

You may be in Britain for the Roman high life, but why limit yourself just to the parts of these islands that fall under Roman sway? If you're not the timorous sort and can handle your own in rough company, you might want to consider heading north of the frontier garrisons and even further afield.

Where the northern frontier lies will depend on when you're visiting of course, and if you're within a few days walk of the army posts you will still likely find something of the southern mentality and maybe even bump into a Roman patrol checking up on the locals. It's possible you are already starting with trade contacts, such as at the great hill fort of the pugnacious and silver-loving Votadini (Traprain Law). Otherwise, save your trade goods for further away where there's no garrison footprint and these items are scarcer and more valuable. You'll have to make do with tracks rather than roads to get anywhere, so travel sensibly. Unless you have a guide with good local contacts, consider going in armed company if slowed down by carts.

As you travel, take the opportunity to look more closely at the rocks around you. On some of them you may be lucky and chance on some of the strange Pictish artwork occasionally on display. You may also come across it on some of the rudimentary jewellery the locals may try to sell you.

It's rather charming and quite mystical, though you might find after a while if you stay in the one place it can get repetitive. That may have something to do with the way various groups associate themselves with particular images, such as fish, crescents, mirror shapes or sundry wild animals, for instance using bull carvings where it has local religious importance. But where there are a lot of images coming together you can get a real feel for the spirit of the tribes people.

There's also plainer craftswork though. The locals are also reasonable silver smiths and if the local look is your thing, try on a torc as a neck guard. Some of the most striking are made out of chunky chains, making you look as if you've just busted free from an insane royal treasurer's jail.

If you like stone ornaments set in desolate scenery, the far north is for you. There are even hillsides with lots of tiny stones placed on them as if someone has planted baby trolls for crops. Before you run out of mainland, take a diversion to the hinterland and track down the Grey Cairns of Camster. These are long barrows of some forgotten antiquity, but look at the ends and you'll be able to see speaking platforms. Who knows what ancient ceremonies were conducted on them, or recitals of the heroic deeds of the deceased. But such things would be more for tourists in the age of the Pharaohs.

To get to any of the islands you'll obviously need a ship. Thule is the land that is furthest north. It lies close to the frozen area, an area of no animals and barely any plant life, whose people live off such as they can find, and drink beer and mead. But the rains and the lack of sunlight mean they have to grind their corn by hand indoors.

Both sets of northern islands enjoy trade links with the mainland so won't be too surprised to see you, and may even ask to trade in Roman goods by name. In both cases, you'll probably find the best settlements to do trade in focused round what's called a broch. These are rugged towers, round which sometimes you can find clustered compact stone villages. In the near islands, which you can see on a clear day from the tip of the lands of the Picts. Gurness Broch sits right by the waterfront in a northern bay that's home to seals and otters. The settlement is surrounded by ramparts, and is home for around forty families. Each has its own little section, with a separate fireplace and living area, plus separate toilet areas. The furnishings if you look more closely are actually made of stone, even if covered over by vegetation and furs. By the broch itself there's a water tank. You can reach the main tower along what reminds you of a little processional route, and up close you can see it's strongly built, a good eight men high and with walls two or three men thick. But come before the second century to see it at its peak, otherwise you find some small Pictish farm buildings instead. Note the peculiar shape, like a shamrock or clover.

If Orcadia has around a hundred of these brochs, there are more on the more distant islands. Mousa Broch is one, perched again on the shoreline of one of the smaller islands. It stands about seven men high, looking slightly bent and misshapen like a cast off misfired pot, or the nape of a knee. Within its hugely thick walls are a number of storage rooms. The stairwell is steep and narrow and takes you to an upper level and to the top, from where you can look over the sea and keep an eye on your boat.

You might consider these useful tips when travelling beyond Roman territory;
• The far north has some striking clothing. There are textiles woven in a check pattern; woollen hoods with knotted strings dangling down; and hats made from the plant fibres of hair moss that look like a pointy basket. These can make interesting gifts for friends back home.

• Some people live in crannogs, or wooden buildings actually built on lakes. These are harder to assault.

• Wood is at a premium here. Even on the Roman border, seasoned timber is considered a valuable commodity, and once you get up to the islands trees are small and rare. Look out for the local cups made out of a vertebra from a whale, with their jaunty long handles sticking out, or chopping boards made from bones. Nearer the border there are many large and ancient trees, big enough to make kegs out of a single slice of bough. Oak is favoured for being tough, alder for being carved, and willow and hazel because they are flexible. But don't expect the locals to have the same skill set – or hand-turned bow lathes – of their Roman counterparts when looking for goods.

• Torcs are popular. They come in different designs – twisted gold ribbons made locally; hammered raised designs once imported from Gaul; and intricate wire designs like gold braid, crafted with Roman skill.

• Near the border, Roman coins are valid. But beyond the immediate trading area bronze becomes worthless and it's more a question of silver weight. Trading on the border, take up quality goods and exchange for grain and hides. We suggest selling ear rings, tweezers, games and horse fittings – in the far north they have to make even horse bridles out of bone. Bronze table ware and wine strainers can make good gifts if you need to impress a local chieftain first. Some people like tiny moustache combs.

• Recycle. Broken glass this far north gets melted down and reshaped. Multipatterned and multicoloured globules of it are called 'eyeballs'. Even Samian bowls can have bits cut out and reused, or fragments can be used to polish items with.

Instead of travelling north, you can head in the other direction in the Low Season and try heading for little Britain. Just as various Saxon colonies have been springing up on the Gallic coast (look for place names with a -hem at the end of them), so too can you find settlers coming from closer ports. Armorica is that part of Gaul which, in the latest part of the Low Season, has been increasingly colonised by Britons leaving their homeland.

But that's a subject for another day. You can find out more about these communities in Smelling Attila's Battleground; Smoking Franks and Sense, at all good scroll stockists.

There is also the option of quitting Britain and sailing out to its neighbouring island. We sadly know little as to its peoples and customs. Of Hibernia we are informed the strange notions that its inhabitants eat their dead fathers, chew grass, and sleep with their close female relatives. However, this is just hearsay as told to Roman historians. The locals may be even more terrifying.

Northern Hibernia

Few and far between are the tales that reach Roman lands of the lives and peoples of Hibernia. Many things are rumoured, some outlandish, others perhaps true. It is perhaps safest simply to note that its peoples are Celts, and as such must bear many similarities (perhaps sometimes superficially) with the forgotten pasts of their cousins in Britannia, with whom they share a closely related but very distinct language.

We have been told by a most roundabout route, however, a detail which may be of some small use to travellers. It concerns the dwellings of these folk, and how they can be divided into two types. There is the rath. And there is the cashel.

The rath is a form of small fort, perhaps on elevated ground, with surrounding turf walls and ditch creating an outer rampart. Some in the south and west are said to have inner chambers dug in, though our source was unable to confirm this. Inside the walls sit homesteads. It provides a homely refuge from casual dangers.

A cashel is a more serious enterprise. Though at a casual

An Irish rath is a good place to stop. With luck you will find a local chief who wants to hire you as a bodyguard. The pay is good.
(c) Northern Ireland Environment Agency

glance it appears similar to a rath, it is in fact made of stone, and quite possibly marks the dwelling of a person of some local importance and where he'll stash his cattle. As time goes on they'll both become almost something of a craze.

Notes for out-of-season travellers

Drumena Cashel is a State Care site managed by the Environment Agency in Northern Ireland, and can be visited by the public. The department's web site gives some information on sites:
http://www.doeni.gov.uk/niea/places_to_visit_home
DOENI also has a database and web mapping on line, where people can get a lot more detail on their sites -
http://www.doeni.gov.uk/niea/other-index/content-databases/content-databases-ambit.htm and
http://maps.ehsni.gov.uk/MapViewer/Default.aspx.
Readers may also be interested in exploring a number of books on Northern Irish archaeology. Deer Park Farms by Chris Lynn and Jackie McDowell describes in detail the excavation of the rath near Glenarm. There are also Hidden History Below our Feet: The Archaeological Story of Belfast by Ruari Ó Baoill ; Archaeological Objects from County Fermanagh by Brian Williams and Sarah Gormley; and NIEA's A Guide to the Historic Monuments of Northern Ireland in State Care. Ulster Museum in Belfast is certainly worth a visit for its Iron Age collection.

Good luck with your visit. We hope you have a fantastic stay. But remember...

The Roman Empire isn't going to last forever. Start planning your visit now to avoid missing out on a trip of a lifetime. Delay too long and before you know it, you're looking at rubble and carrion and wondering where on earth the fun times went. Five star resorts are a thing of memory.

We say however, that pillaging isn't just for life, it's for Christmas. Get across and raiding those homesteads while there's decent loot still to be had. And mind the tiling at places like these if you are a roaming Saxon squatter: it could drop off and get you killed.

Emergency Latin

Travelling in foreign parts can raise all manner of difficulties in communication. Here are some handy phrases you can turn to in an emergency, courtesy of our friend Josephus the rhetor of the children of the Spaldingas tribe.

DIC, AGE: QUO IN LOCO MEUM CURRUM RELINQUERE POSSUM?

Excuse me. Where can I park my chariot?

EMERE VELIM DONUM UXORI, QUAE DOMI MANET.

I'd like to buy a gift for my wife back home

HOC OLUS, QUALE EST?

What manner of vegetable is that

HAEC RES, QUANTI EST?

How much is this thing?

DA MIHI, AGE, DECEM ASSES PRO HOC DENARIO?

Do you have change for a denarius?

SPECTA HUNC DENARIUM; NON CORRUPTUS EST.

I think you'll find it is not a forgery

CAUDEX! MANUS TUAS ADIME MIHI!

Take your hands off me you blockhead

LEGATUS BATAVIORUM MIHI CONSULENDUS EST DE HAC INIURIA.

I demand to see the Batavian ambassador

HAEC PECUNIA TUA ERIT, SI OBLITUS ERIS TE ME VIDISSE.

Take this money. You didn't see me, right?
MORIETUR CATULUS SI QUID TU FACERE CONATUS ERIS.
One false move and the puppy gets it
FLOCCI NON FACIO. HAEC SCAPHA MIHI MUTUANDA EST.
I don't give a fig. I need to borrow this small boat
PER IOVEM MARTEMQUE, DEDITE VOS VESTRAQUE SI VIVERE
VULTIS!
By the gods of thunder and of war I demand you surrender
this town in return for your pathetic lives
NISI GLADIUM MANU EMITTES, CAPUT AMITTES.
Drop your sword or say goodbye to your noggin
OMNIA AUREA DEMITTITE IN HANC URNAM QUAE PRAEBITA
EST!
Please place all the gold in the buckets provided
GRATIAS VOBIS AGO QUOD OPTIME HOSPITIO VESTRO USUS SUM.
Thank you for making our visit so enjoyable

Greek phrases you may need
Εν τή Βρεττανία βαλαντιοτομούσιν;
En te Brettania balantiotomousin?
Are there pickpockets in Britain?
Ο.ι. μοί! Φαίνομαι έχων δόρυ τί εν τώ σκελεί.
Oimoi ! Phainomai echon doru ti en to skelei.
Alas, I seem to have a spear in my leg.
Αλλά τό τραύμα μόνον εν τη σαρκί εστίν.
Alla to trauma monon en te sarki estin.
It is just a flesh wound.
Πρός δέ τούτοις, δέομαι ολίγης τινός αλοιφής.
Δυσμενής γάρ εστί
η κατάστασις εμού.
Pros de toutois deomai oliges tinos aloiphes. Dusmenes gar
esti e katastasis emou.
In addition I need some ointment. For I have an unfortunate
condition.

Κατανοέω, λάμβανε ταύτην τήν αλοιφήν ἅπαξ καθημέραν.

Katanoeo, lambane tauten ten aloiphen apax kathemeron.

I understand; use this ointment once daily.

Λάβε τόν οβολόν τούτον. Ευχαριστώ σοί.

Labe ton obolon touton. Eucharisto soi.

Have this coin. Thank-you.

About the author

Dr Lee Rotherham is by background a linguist, historian, author, political agitator and occasional soldier. Having written widely on EU affairs and on government waste, he here returns to his academic roots after being serially impressed by the evocative illustrations on display boards at numerous historical sites, particularly those commissioned by English Heritage where he once briefly worked.

According to his university head of department, after years of study his Latin reached the dizzying heights of being as good as an average semi-literate auxiliary stuck out on Hadrian's Wall. Despite occasionally practising it on church memorials and as a medium of last resort with hilltop foreign clergy, he has mostly forgotten even this pitiful level and cannot be relied on in any diplomatic incident involving the Vatican.

Acknowledgements

Identifying illustrations that could be used in the book proved to be a far more daunting task than originally anticipated, involving many hundreds of emails. The author would like to thank the many people who assisted patiently with this, particularly in councils' museums and information services. In addition to those individuals attributed in the main text, particular thanks must go to those who suggested alternative sources and helped obtain permissions. These include Phil Cooper at Surrey County Council; Gary Brown, Dr Frank Meddens and Victoria Ridgeway at Pre-Construct

Archaeology; Richard de Peyer at Wycombe Museum; Gail Pollock at DOENI; Amy Moffat and Brian Philp at Crofton Roman villa; Dave Allen at Hants County Council; Laura Hadland at Leicester Arts and Museum Service; Margaret Lound at Castleford and District Historical Society; Mike Codd; Ruth Stratton and Rob Bandy at Stevenage Museum; Keith Fitzpatrick-Matthews; Karen Snowden; Ivan Lapper; Richard Cross of Canterbury Council; Philip Hadland and Canterbury City Museums; Moya Watson and Cheshire Archaeology Advisory Planning Service; David Rice and Gloucester Museums Service; Andrew Hutchinson; Peter Rowe of Tees Archaeology; Paul Jones and the Glamorgan-Gwent Archaeological Trust; John Fletcher and the Isle of Wight Heritage Service; Fiona Watson and the Vindolanda Trust; David Evans and South Gloucs Council; Alison Bennett and Essex County Council; Nick Wickenden of Chelmsford Council; Roy and Liz Friendship-Taylor and the Upper Nene Archaeological Society; and Jane Elder and Canterbury Archaeological Trust.

Especial thanks to Joe Millington for help with the emergency phrases, and thanks to Valentina Fori for assistance with the unusual Greek.

I should also in particular like to thank up-and-coming artist Laura Haines, Her models are from a group called Vicus: members re-enact ancient Britain from daily life through legionaries to gladiatorial scraps. If you want to watch them at work, or even fancy joining the XXth Legion, have a look at http://www.vicus.org.uk.

Those interested in viewing more of Laura's remarkable work can view her website www.laurahaines.co.uk, or follow her blog at http://laura-randomscribblings.blogspot.co.uk/ She herself can be contacted (and commissioned) at info@laurahaines.co.uk
My aim in writing this book has been to encourage an interest in the vestiges of our past, often at first sight little more than stumpy walls, but also in the professions and projects associated with heritage work today.